A Heart For Jesus

Thomas D. Hall

Order this book online at www.trafford.com
or email orders@trafford.com

Most Trafford titles are also available at major online book retailers.

Print information available on the last page.

ISBN: 978-1-4120-4060-0 (sc)
ISBN: 978-1-4122-2905-0 (e)

Trafford rev. 10/27/2021

www.trafford.com

North America & international
toll-free: 844-688-6899 (USA & Canada)
fax: 812 355 4082

Contents

Introduction

*Study Questions
Small group study guide will follow at the end of each chapter!

Dedication

I stand in awe, at Gods sovereign majesty and grace. I dedicate this book to the Lord, in the humble hope that I may somehow reflect his glory. I pray that you will see God, the author and perfecter of my faith, in this book, not me. Without the grace and love of Christ, I would be dead in my sins.

To my loving wife, whose encouragement and patience made this book a reality!

Introduction

When I think of my most troubled times in my life I always wanted to reach out for help, to my parents, to my friends, or to something that would make me feel better. As I began to grow up, I started to reach for other things. Even though I was raised in a church, I never really understood God and what he was all about. I never understood that what I needed was in my heart all along. I never thought, was taught, or heard that all I needed to do was look inside my heart to find a relationship with Jesus. I truly believed that God loved me when I was good and he did not love me when I was bad. So I thought, I had better be good if I wanted God to love me.

My journey to health, healing, wholeness, and direction has been documented in this book. I truly believe that I have found the "peace" that God in Christ Jesus provides. During the past few years, I have felt a most powerful call from God to share my journey with you. In my waking hours and in my dreams, in my work and in my study of God's word, the idea of Testimony has both compelled and disabled me. Through my personal study of the Book of Acts, I began to hear God's call on my life in a most powerful way. I already knew, God had saved me for his purposes, but I could not quite hear or possibly was not ready to hear his calling in my life. Throughout the Book of Acts, testimony and witnessing are the common threads, the Acts of the Apostles, that proclaim the truth of Jesus Christ. Without their work, the Church would not have evolved. They stepped out in faith against much greater odds than I will ever face in my life. Through the study of Acts, my journey became apparent to me. God spoke to me through his word, and the Holy Spirit has compelled me to share my life, specifically for God's higher purpose!

I am calling out to all men, women, teens and children who are suffering in the bondage of their own addictions and self-loathing. I am calling out to all those who do not have a church home. I am calling out to all those who do not have a small group within their current church home. I am calling out to all those who do not know the blessings of being saved, by grace through faith, for the works of service. I am calling out to all those who have had their idea of what church should be, crushed, and have chosen to withdraw from church and possibly God. I am calling out to all believers who are persistent in the faith, but do not understand their nature in Christ and may be spiritually lost. I am calling out to all those who desire to know God better but are spiritually ignorant as to the magnitude of Christ's work on the Cross and how it relates to their lives. Finally, I am calling to all those who scoff, to those who are nonbelievers.

My message is clear and the implications are life changing: You do not have to walk alone anymore. You do not have to be dead in your sins and addictions anymore! Yes, you too can be made alive in Christ; you too, can know the peace and joy of a fruitful life, you too can live out of grace and learn to harness the "spirit of power" that God through Christ Jesus provides.

Cry out to God, invite Jesus into your heart, and welcome him home! Look in the mirror, see the problem, then ask God to help you remove the defects of character that reside in your heart. Challenge yourself to renew your mind and your attitudes, seek God and the protection of his Holy armor, while he may be found. Call upon God while he is near. Let Christ justify you in his grace and heal your spirit. Begin to understand who we are in Christ and what we are called to be! Learn to grow in the knowledge of God by seeking his word. Seek his word and know the truth. Share the truth of his word, and build up the body of Christ, so that his word may accomplish the purpose for which he sent it. Understand that we will be set apart by God's word and that by sharing his word, it will not return to him empty, but in fact will accomplish the purpose for which he sent it!

Chapter 1

My Story!

I wish I could describe to you how difficult this part of my journey is. What part you may ask? The part where I have to tell you who I was, how bad things got in my life, and what it took for me to find God. You see I would rather you just know me as a warrior for the Christian Heart! The fact remains that to get a clear picture of the magnitude of Gods grace you must dive deep into the utter despair that clouded my fruitless existence. It is imperative that you comprehend Gods design, he is the author of my life, he loves me so much that he gave me the freedom to choose the person I wanted to be. As my story and this book unfold I hope you will firmly grasp the idea of our God given free will, the fundamental premise that God loves us so much that he lets us go free to choose who we want to be, which road we will travel in this life and ultimately where our spirits will reside. Will we choose God or the world? After all what is true love if it is not freely chosen. In my journey I have made many woefully deficient choices in my life that gave way to personal tragedies. It is my desire to help you see the magnitude of what is at stake when we fail to recognize who we are in Christ and how we live out of the gift of grace that Christ placed in our hearts when we are given a clean heart and a fresh start. So, let us begin!

A Little Background

In my heart's desire as a child I wanted primarily to be liked, to be a part of the group, any group. I was the second of three brothers and had a much younger sister who was born when I was thirteen. I was big for my age, a bit overweight, very

7

clumsy, and completely lost when it came to a sense of self-worth or self-esteem. At a young age, I got into all types of mischief and trouble. I am not sure what led me that way. Maybe it was a cry for attention. Doubtful, though, I was just plain mischievous. I have had many explanations offered to me, yet I have never clung to any one in particular, because they all placed blame on someone else for my actions. Most all outside counseling I have taken in my adult years has wanted me to find fault with someone else in order that I may be in some strange fashion freed from the pains of my childhood. Could it be that I was the middle brother and got overlooked, could it be that my father worked hard long hours to provide so well for us, could it be that my mother and I did not get along well as I grew up, or could it be that this was God's will for my life.

I missed the call!

I believe that at a very young age, God calls us into a relationship with him, and I believe I missed that call. Let me jump forward a bit to explain. As I have grown in my journey with Christ, I have learned to better identify and discern the promptings of the Holy Spirit. As a Christian man, I do believe that God responds to our prayers, our cries and pleas for help. The key to understanding his response to our cries is threefold.

"Be still, and know that I am God." (NIV)
— Psalm 46:10

First, it is imperative that we learn how to be still and quiet, and in so doing honor God for his sovereign majesty and power. Before we can hear what God has to say to us, we must learn to humbly bow down before him and exalt him.

"If you had responded to my rebuke, I would have poured out my heart to you and made my thoughts known to you." (NIV)
— Proverbs 1:23

8

Second, once we have humbled ourselves and learned to be still and quiet before him, we must then take on the task of listening. Yes, I said listen. How difficult it is for us, currently, to do these two things. In order for us to hear what it is that God is saying to us, we must take the cotton out of our ears and put it in our mouths. Solomon is telling us in the above-referenced passage that God wants to make his ways known to us, but we must be willing to remove that selfish pride that says my ways, my thoughts, and my ideas are higher than God's. We must put away our sinful pride and be willing to listen. Discernment of God's will and way for me in any particular circumstance can come in many forms. Most often, I feel it in my quiet time through the promptings of the Holy Spirit, in my soul. Oftentimes when I do not hear or feel anything, God is asking me to remain faithful and patient, and trust that his will, will be made known to me in his time, not mine. I must learn patience and the practice of waiting on God. Often, I will be in one of my God-centered small groups and through listening to others, I will hear God's will as he speaks through others.

"Blessed is the man who does not walk in the counsel of the wicked, or stand in the way of sinners, or sit in the seat of mockers. But his delight is in the law of the Lord and on his law he meditates day and night. He is like a tree planted by streams of water, which yields its fruit in season and whose leaf does not whither. Whatever he does prospers."
— Psalm 1:1-3

Third, is the idea that in order for us to understand God we must know him better. The only real way to know him better is to meditate on his word. This means that we must literally each day set apart time where we will study a handful of verses or a chapter of his word. Once read, we must then begin to chew on it, study it, comprehend it, and memorize it. Picture the image of a person who chews on his meat. Does he take the bite

9

and swallow it? No, he chews on it, to absorb the flavor and benefit from the nutrients that the meat has to offer, and enjoy the pleasure that it brings. In the same way, God is calling us to know him better by chewing on his word.

The point is, no matter what circumstance you are in, if you want to hear and discern the will and way of God, you must be still before God, then we must patiently listen for his wisdom and finally we must meditate upon his word.

Back to My Story

I believe God was calling me into a relationship with him as a child. I recall many times as a preteen where I had a hunger for something all-powerful and peaceful. During those times alone, I would feel my soul hungering for something. I can remember the feeling as being one similar to hunger pains. My soul was crying out for a relationship with God, but I mistook it for hunger or growing pains. I look back today and see it as a critical turning point in my life. I believe that if I had had the knowledge or interest or had been willing to listen to what was said about God at a younger age that things might have been different for me.

For this reason, it is so very important to me that my children go to church and stay involved in youth activities and that, as a father, I must keep them focused on God and what the relationship is about. Yes, possibly things could have been different for me if I had been able to understand those feelings some twenty-five to thirty years ago, but more importantly, I believe that God's design for my life was purposeful. God has a special purpose for my life and yours. He wants me to witness for him of the incredible transformation that can take place in a person's heart when you give your life to Christ.

God Saved Me from Myself

Do not be fooled, miracles did not occur only in the Bible. I too, am a miracle! God saved me from myself! I believe that the experiences of my childhood were a design by God to prepare me for a relationship that would come many years down the road. I believe God has been with me from the very beginning and he has watched me struggle as a child, as a teenager, as a cocky, gambling, alcoholic, drug meddling young man. Then as an immature adult still caught up in his childish ways, as a struggling alcoholic and addict who became chronically hopeless, to a person who had developed chronic eating disorders as a result of alcohol and drug abuse, to a completely broken man who had become of his own accord, hopelessly lost in the things of this world. Through my failures I found victory in Christ. Ultimately, God's goal for all of his children is to bring us into his family. God saw this miracle through in my life!

Who am I and why am I sharing my story?

I am one of many hundreds of thousands of people out there who has or may still be traveling down the same road of addiction, isolation, self-hatred, spiritual ignorance, and misunderstanding of our spiritual nature as I did. Yes, today, I am a miracle, a child of God, saved by the grace of my redeemer, Jesus Christ. I want to witness to those who are lost, those who do not understand God, to those who fear church and all the gifts associated with serving God. To those who do not understand who they are in Christ and what it means to be saved. To those who are caught in the bondage of any type of addiction; alcohol, drugs, eating disorders, pornography, gossip, gambling, etc. To those who do not understand their spiritual nature. To anyone, whatever your personal failures may be, we all have them and if we allow them to, they will keep us from God. We need to understand that Christ is the answer and the beginning of transformation is a matter of your heart.

Change is rooted in the truth and change begins when we ask Jesus to come into our hearts and we humbly turn our hearts, our will, and our lives over to the care of God. It is a humble admission of powerlessness that says, "God; I believe that Jesus died for my sins, I believe that Jesus is your son and my holy savior, I hear your promise, please come into my heart and heal me!" So, what is the truth? I intend to identify that in this text!

"For it is by grace that you have been saved, through faith — and this not from yourselves, it is a gift of God — not by works, so that no one can boast."
— Ephesians 2:8-9

My personality is that by nature, I am a sinner, with an overindulgent addictive personality type. I have been referred to many times as an egomaniac with an inferiority complex. Why, you may ask? Because before I found Christ I was always worried about myself and what others might think of me, so I was always focusing on my ego or myself. Think about those people who are always talking about themselves, their problems, and their pain. Are they not caught up in their own foolish pride? This is where I was in my addictions, always thinking about me and never focusing on others. I was an egomaniac. Then, to make matters worse I never felt I amounted to much of anything, I always felt less than for some reason, I always felt as though I did not measure up. Thus, I had an inferiority complex most of the time.

My Testimony:

Since my childhood, I can remember an emptiness that resided inside of me. I never knew what that emptiness was. I have traveled many roads searching for peace, trying to find anything that would fill that void. My search has taken me down many roads. On these roads, I encountered many warning signs.

Eventually I ignored those signs and I ended up in places that only God could restore me from. My search was always on the outside, trying to find something to drink, to smoke, to eat, to use, or to buy, someone to love, anything that I could project my budding man hood on that would help me to feel whole. Throughout this journey, I could never find the missing "peace" for which I was searching. The only things I found that helped at all only created temporary satisfaction and escape. Those temporary fixes became my state of mind and I clung to them until I could no longer live without them. I followed these compulsions to death's door, through financial ruin, vehicle repossessions, loss of home, health, integrity, marriage, love, and the loss of respect for self and from family and friends.

The most painful part of the process came when I could no longer stand to see the man I had become. I finally realized I was in deep trouble when I looked in the mirror one morning. What I saw made me cry! I could not stand to look at the person I had become. The person staring back at me was not the true spirit God created me to be. Sin defined is the disparity between who God created me to be and the person that I am. At that point, in my life, I realized that I was sin.

I had become my will, an excruciatingly painful glimpse of what a person is capable of doing to himself when he lacks a good orderly direction in life (G.O.D.), when a person follows his will instead of God's word. A place where self-will is so rampant that it invades the very core of your being. When the desires for the pleasures of this world are so chronically pursued that loss of life, family, home, integrity, and character make no difference. Where there is a lack of sensible reasoning, a corruption of the mind. A place where moral decay is rampant and our minds are rotted by the impure thoughts and concoctions that are consumed by our flesh. Lust, gluttony, greed, sloth, envy, anger, and pride were the sole motivators of my excruciatingly painful existence. In this state of moral decay, impulsive action breeds an inherent compulsion to continue in sin. Yes, I was dead in my sins, helplessly floundering in the lake of fire. A place where shame, guilt, self-hatred and remorse twist any thread of moral fiber that remains, into crippling bouts of self-loathing and paralyzing fear.

Fear becomes the motivator of the spiritually lost. Acting on many types of fear, the fear of failure, the fear of being found out for what I truly had become, the fear of losing what little I had left, the fear of getting too close to anyone because they might see who I really was.

Oh, but to wade in the waters of impending doom, to bask in the deep darkness of utter despair, to cry out for help to some sort of God for relief, from the chains of addiction which securely fastened me to the gates of hell. To live a daily life caught up in the sickening disease of worry, a perverse and faithless existence equal to that of trying to climb a steep muddy embankment during torrential rains. I was never able to cool the fire that burned inside of me. The mountain of worries and waves of impending doom continued to ripple through my chaotic mind.

One after another the worries, fears, and transgressions mount. The fear of being found out and shame of who you have become keeps you from reaching out. Paradoxically, Satan kept me swimming in the lake of fire, by twisting my pride and teasing my mind with the insanely irrational idea that tomorrow will be a new day. If I can just get through today, I will not do this again tomorrow!

Then a prayerful bargain is offered. "God, please help me get through this and I promise I will not do that." The new dawn arrives along with a sweeping feeling of impending doom. Fears of what you did the night before consume you. Then out of nowhere it hits, the seething jaws of craving clench their teeth around your soul and refuse to let go, coaxing you, calling you, beckoning you back to the lake of fire and off I went, with little fight left in me, doomed again to repeat the menacing insanity that had invaded my person. I was not the man God made me to be; I was sin in the flesh. I simply reflected worldly values.

As my disease worsened, I began to cry out for relief from the bondage of self only to return to my closet of despair, as my flesh would will it. I began to know a craving that besieged all desires, a seductive aching of the inner workings of my brain that would beckon me. It would call me into any form of depravity to soothe its desire. A craving for things that I knew would soon kill me, but of myself, I could not resist the impulse.

Yes, the deepest, darkest side of addiction is the continual choice to act on it when death looms inevitable. The Apostle Paul describes this painful existence in Ephesians 4:17-19;

"So, I tell you this, and insist on it in the Lord, that you most no longer live as the Gentiles do, in the futility of their thinking. They are darkened in their understanding and separated from the life of God because of the ignorance that is in them due to the hardening of their hearts. Having lost all sensitivity, they have given themselves over to sensuality so as to indulge in every kind of impurity, with a continual lust for more." (NIV)

As a child, I had all the gifts of childhood, wonderful parents, brothers, sisters, private school education, country club memberships, but the bondage of addiction and the sin of self-absorption and uncontrollable weakness knew no boundaries. As an early teen I found myself constantly comparing my insides to your outsides, the net result always being the same: I was not good enough, I was too fat, too short, too ugly, not rich enough, not fast enough. Every time I went into a room, I felt less than and then I found alcohol. At the age of twelve, I had my first drink. It did two things for me:

15

- It broke through the hard outer shell of inferiority that I struggled with and gave me courage; yes, I found courage in the bottle, and
- It temporarily filled that hole inside me that could not find peace.

My spirit, the heart of my inner being, was crying out for a relationship with God, and it was covered with alcohol, a temporary fix that would leave me in a constant state of dissatisfaction, always wanting more, never being able to relive the euphoria of the first hit.

Little did I know that it would take some fifteen years to begin a search to understand what that missing "peace" was in my life? I spent the rest of my high school days working, playing sports, and having fun drinking. I was a hard worker and received several awards in sports. As I turned eighteen and left for college I had a high opinion of myself and thought the world was mine. As I left for college my life was scary, to say the least. I will never forget that day I left home. You see, my parents had been divorced for many years and my mom and I had been through many a conflict together. We were continually at odds over my wants and desires and what she new was best for me. As a teenager, I could not hear nor did I want to hear the voice of reason or wisdom. For same insane reason I always felt she was just trying to control me.

Personal Testimony about My Mother and I

As a child, my father was my world to me and my mother could not win for losing. I gravitated toward my father and I wanted to be just like him. When my parents divorced, I lived with my mother and I know I was painfully difficult to handle. From the time, I was fourteen until I left for college I was always getting into trouble and my mother and I fought. Mom, I am

16

sorry for all the times I hurt you, lashed out at you, and spoke unkind words to you. Thank you for loving me enough to teach me right from wrong even though I would not hear it at the time. You trained me up in the way I needed to go and even though I did not heed it, I have returned to it.

My mother and I did not see much of each other over the next several years. Some brief time at holidays and possibly a few phone calls. Little did she know or could have known the path my feet had journeyed upon. I was quick to keep my shortcomings hidden from her and tried to avoid her getting too close to me. Between the ages of, eighteen and twenty-seven I kept my mother at a distance as I became more entrenched in my troubled ways. My mother knew I was in trouble, but it was not until I had lost everything and I was willing to help myself that she returned to help me to my feet again.

Yes, I had lost everything and had become, morally, physically, spiritually, and financially bankrupt. It was during those trials that she expressed tough love and would not let me manipulate her when I was in a bad way. She did not help me or give me money when I was not trying to help myself. Only now, being a parent myself of two wonderful children can I begin to relate to the degree of pain she must have felt as she watched me slowly destroy myself.

My mother was steadfast in her love. She would not help me until she saw that I was truly ready to help myself! My mother was an angel in the darkest hours of my life. How could she have ever known that after so many false attempts to clean up my life, I was finally serious? How could she have known that I was finally beaten into submission with my old ways? How could she have known that this time was the right time for her to say, "OK, I will help you"?

I have always known she had faith in God but I never understood it. I have always known that she entrusted the care of her life to God but could not comprehend it. Yes, after she suffered through all the painful things I created, she remained there ready to help, but only when I was ready to change. The grace and love that my mom offered me at the lowest point in my life is the kind of grace and love that God in Christ Jesus provides! In the same way, Jesus is waiting for us to knock so that he can offer us the grace that only our Lord Jesus can provide through the Cross. The grace that says you are justified by what I did for you on the Cross, now go repent and sin no more. God's grace offers health, healing, wholeness, and direction!

Back to My Story

That infamous morning in my memory came sooner than I cared to admit. As I packed my luggage to go, I also packed up my childhood. My mother was being remarried and moving to Tennessee, my dad was living in a condominium, and our house was sold. Essentially my life as I knew it had ended, it was over and finished. I would never return home nor did I know where home would be.

I packed my car and began the walk to say goodbye to my mom. I was driving 450 miles away to attend college. I was very fearful, as I did not know to where I was going or really how to get there. When I reached my mom's room to say goodbye, she was sitting down putting her makeup on. I could tell my mother was struggling and even in the midst of our respective brokenness, we both fought back the tears. We were both beginning new lives and neither one of us really knew when we would see each other again. It was a painfully difficult departure for me as I hid my tears from her. When I drove away from my childhood home, my tears flowed uncontrollably. I realized that I was on my own; everything that I had known was over, finished, and done! I had no roots left and the next place I planted my roots did not bear any fruit.

By the middle of my second year in college, I had experimented with drugs and gambling, and had started skipping classes to party. During football season of my sophomore year in college, I got involved in gambling. I lost a lot of money, many thousands of dollars. I had no way to pay it back and I was in serious trouble. I summoned the courage to call my father for help. When we spoke I told him of my plight and his response was what I can only imagine must have been the hardest thing in the world for a father to tell his son. He said, "Son, you got yourself into it, you're going to have to get yourself out."

I was angry and scared to death. I wanted to end my life. I truly contemplated the idea of killing myself because money was so hard to come by, and I saw no way out. I will never ever forget lying in my bed wanting to end my life and never once thinking about God and prayer. Somehow, I forged ahead. I was already working one job to help pay my way through college and took on two more jobs and struck a deal to pay the money back as quickly as I could. Soon, I could no longer keep up the pace of the three jobs and school and I quit going altogether. The people I owed the money to saw me drop out of college to pay them off and I guess that somehow they appreciated that. Each day when I finished work I would stop by and give them the tips I had made from delivering food and bartending. They allowed me to keep what I needed to live. I will never forget the call I got one night as I was cooking. It went like this. "We see you are really working hard to pay us off and we appreciate that. We want to offer you an opportunity to pay this off quicker. It involves something illegal and you could get in trouble if you were caught. You could make hundreds of dollars per night, if you are interested." They were offering me an opportunity to get involved with selling drugs to pay them back.

19

This was a turning point in my life, I knew it was one of those decisions that would possibly prove to be fatal, but for some reason, maybe a momentary lack of sound reasoning, I was desperate and I accepted. I must have become addicted to the drinking and the drugs somewhere in the next few months.

Money, guns, bookies, parties, quick trips to the Bahamas, buying motorcycles, and cool audiovisual stuff became the order of the day. I was constantly partying, dropped out of college, and went to work in the family business promoting concerts. I was highly successful with my father's line of work and made a lot of money fast. This lifestyle fueled my addiction. I was married to my high school and college girlfriend at age twenty-three and within a year, she was ready to leave me. I will never forget that turning point in my life and the look on her face. It was when I said goodbye to any possibility of sanity or healthy relationships and chose to drink and drug in the seclusion of my apartment without anyone around to interfere in my addictions.

The next three years of my life were unfathomably demoralizing for me. I tried daily to stop my addiction. I would swear it off, bargain with God, but within a few hours, I was doing it all over again. I hated who I had become. I could not keep food down and I had bleeding ulcers. I was stripped first of my home, then my vehicles, then personal financial bankruptcy. Moral and spiritual bankruptcy had occurred long ago. Those last three years of my life, before I found Christ, I wasted in hiding, doing the very things I am too ashamed to admit to, until now. I spent weeks locked up in my apartment and or hotels; I was arrested several times, slept in my car, and did what I had to do to get by. At this point in my life, I could not look in the mirror because I would sob uncontrollably. The bondage of addiction was so intensely fierce that I acted on the cravings without regard to others or myself. I was chained to my sinful, self-loathing, and self-indulgence. I hated myself and the personal hell I had created. At this point in my journey, I was firm in my belief that God did not want anything to do with me.

In my final bout with alcohol and drugs before my entering a treatment center, I had been locked up in my apartment for four days. I missed Thanksgiving with my family. I had barricaded my doors and was not responding to the many phone calls and knocks by worried family and friends. As I entered into that fourth day of sleepless hell, I began to feel incredibly sick, having been up the entire time without food or sleep, only alcohol and drugs in my system, my heart began to race uncontrollably. I knew I was headed for another overdose. As I approached what I felt like was the end, I thought about God briefly, I thought about my family briefly, and then I caught a glimpse of the remaining drugs and liquor by the bed and in that fleeting moment I chose death in my disease. Yes, I chose to continue doing the very thing that was killing me at that moment. The next thing I remember was waking up in a hospital. I remember seeing my mother by my bed with tears in her eyes. I can only imagine the pain she must have felt, not to mention the complete and utter helplessness.

About a week later, I was released from the hospital to the care of my mother and counselor. These two women loved me when I could not love myself. Sophie was my counselor free of charge! You see, as a twenty-seven-year-old man I was not capable of living alone or taking care of myself. I knew, the doctors knew, and my family knew that if I were left on my own I would die. After all, I had been able to convince family members and doctors several other times that I was OK, that I could take care of myself.

As a twenty-seven-year-old man, I could not keep my phone or power on, my apartment was a disaster zone, I spent every waking hour doing drugs, stealing to get alcohol and drugs, or plotting how and whom I would have to manipulate to get what I needed. I had sold everything of any value to get what I needed. I did not have a valid license or legal vehicle, but I would drive anyway. I had lost any self-respect in accordance with personal care and hygiene. I was a petty thief, a drunk, a drug addict, I could not keep food down, I would not eat for days then I would gorge only to throw it up again. I had no money, no self-respect, no faith, no love left; I was completely beaten by the very thing that had given me courage fourteen years before.

For me alcohol was the beginning, and I always said I would never cross that line, but I did. I crossed every line I swore I would not, always seeking something that was not attainable. The second hit never would be as good as the first and it never was the same. The insanity of it all was that I knew where I would end up when I picked it up, yet somehow my mind beckoned me back and in my sickness, I somehow believed it would be different each time.

So there, I lay in the bedroom of my mother's home, her twenty-seven-year-old son who could not be trusted to live alone. Waxing rivers of tears and toiling in waves of self-loathing. As I cried before God, begging and pleading for his mercy, asking him to save me from my hopeless situation and myself, I reached over and picked up a book my mother left at my bedside. Robert Schuller calls the book God Loves You and So Do I. It told me that God loved me no matter what and that all I had to do was give my heart to Jesus and then by faith believe that he could heal me.

That night I prayed a different prayer. It wasn't "God, if you do this I will do that." It was, "God, I give my life to you, please come into my heart, I need you, please I do not want to die like this. Please, God, save me from myself." As I cried out to God, I felt warmth like never before, the room was filled with a bright light, and the sunlight of the Holy Spirit filled my room that night. I felt Jesus touch my heart that night. He said, "I love you and I will take care of you, you do not have to live like this any more." That was over twelve years ago. I slept on and off that night and soon after; I drove to a treatment center in Atlanta. Yes, by myself, in a car my mother helped me to get. I spent twenty-three days there. I went through some difficult withdrawals and after about five days, I began to start hearing about learning to live all over again. They taught me to start at the very beginning. I had to learn to respect other people's property, to practice personal hygiene, to manage my finances. They took me to AA and NA meetings where I met other recovering alcoholics and drug addicts who were living a life of recovery and walking with God. I began to hunger for a new life with God and that old fire I remembered, as a teenager, began to burn in me again. The desire to make something out of my life began to outdistance the sinful cravings of my flesh. I was ready to change!

I have been clean for over twelve years now, by God's grace. God has given me gifts beyond my wildest dreams as I have hungered to know him better! I have had tremendous successes and many failures in my journey. The difference this time is that in my failures I know God was with me and he was trying to teach me to get up and continue to walk in faith. God has taught me to reflect his glory in all that I do. I am blessed with a relationship with Jesus, A Heart for Jesus, love, family, church, friends, a business partner, a business, and plenty of wonderful clients.

Wow, you may be thinking, why would anyone want to tell the world about these horrible events in his life? What will people think? Well, do not think that these thoughts have not crossed my mind to the point of paralysis but scripture rings true at every turn. I have learned this! IT IS NOT ABOUT ME ANYMORE. IT IS ABOUT WHAT GOD HAS DONE IN MY HEART AND WHAT GOD CAN DO IN YOUR HEART. I

KNOW MY PURPOSE IS TO BELIEVE ON JESUS, THE ONE GOD SENT, SERVE THE LORD, AND TO BE A LAMP TO THOSE WHO ARE SEEKING THE LOVE OF CHRIST JESUS. YES, IT IS ABOUT BRINGING AS MANY PEOPLE TO CHRIST AS POSSIBLE. IT IS ABOUT GOD! MY PURPOSE IS TO REFLECT THE IMAGE OF MY CREATOR AND DEVELOP A HEART FOR JESUS!

I will be purposeful in my intent to open up my life to you, as I witness of my walk with Christ, in the coming pages. Please read on, if you want to understand how God sees you, your nature in Christ, what Godly principles you need to develop in your life, and how you can walk through the journey of transformation in Christ with a little less ignorance than I have.

I have often heard it said that religion is for those who have never experienced hell. Spirituality is for those who have been there!

Spirituality has to do with the spirit of God or the human spirit. At the root of the human spirit is our heart. Let us walk together and find out how to have A Heart for Jesus!

Group Study Guide

I pray that men women and teens around the world will open their hearts to the truth of scripture. However, I feel that without a true understanding of our failures and or weaknesses as humans we will not grasp the need to truly know Christ. For this reason I have developed a group study guide. My suggestion is that men and women should have separate study groups. Couples groups are encouraged as well, but I feel like many of our character defects and desires of our sinful nature may not be truly revealed in groups where the opposite sex is present. Please use extra paper if you need. Whatever you do, be thorough and truthful. If we want good results, we must be completely honest.

Question 1: What is your story?

Question 2: Why are you here?

Question 3: How did you come to know Christ?

Chapter 2

The Call to Witness

So this is it, this is why I am writing. I want to witness for Christ, in the humble hope that another person may see Gods glory reflected in my journey. The fact that God would choose to save me from myself when I completely abandoned him still amazes me. In Matthew 9: 13 Jesus said;

"For I did not come to call the righteous, but sinners, to repentance."

I truly believe that I have been saved. I believe that the road to holiness is about allowing Jesus to do his work in our hearts and make us whole, one character flaw at a time. God lifted the compulsive patterns of self-destructive behavior that resided in my heart. God, when humbly asked with a right and sincere heart, restored me to a new beginning.

Over twelve years ago, with much help from others, I realized it was my heart that was suffering so deeply. The emptiness that I had always felt and continued to feel was the distance between my creator and me. The emptiness I felt was not having a relationship with Jesus Christ. The emptiness, I learned, could not be filled with any material possession or substance. I was no longer a pool or a renovation away from success in life, from peace. Only by beginning to develop a relationship with Christ would I begin to heal my heart and my destructive behaviors. My walk with Christ has taken me on a new search to become pure in heart, to develop a true Heart for Jesus.

In Matthew 5:48 Jesus calls us to:

"Be perfect, therefore, as your heavenly Father is perfect."

This is the journey that I want to share with you. I hear it in my sleep; I wake up with the thought of it on my mind. In prayer and meditation, I hear God telling me to witness. Yet, I fight it at every turn. I still fear failure, but I hear God's call on my life and cannot stiff-arm him any longer. To be pure in heart is the goal. This is a tall order and requires continual transformation and growth. This growth or theologically speaking "sanctification" process will last a lifetime and will require an open heart that is prepared to hear, meditate upon, and heed the word of God. It requires a true and tireless act of obedience to a new way of life. A heart that is ready to accept change as a constant and walk through it in faith. This calling to be perfect is one that, as a human and a sinner, by nature, we will never completely achieve; however, when we are saved we are born again, we are now winners, not sinners and we have the Holy Spirit as our guide, thus we are called to forge ahead. You see in 2 Corinthians 5:17 Paul tells us:

"Therefore, if anyone is in Christ, he is a new creation; the old has gone, the new has come."

As a new creation in Christ Jesus, we are called to grow, to be like Christ, to let Jesus live out his life through us, while we are here on Earth. Why, you may ask? So that others may see the light of Christ reflected in us, and that God's word, which he sent to us, will not return to him empty! We see ourselves striving to live our lives in the same way Jesus lived. It is the idea that at every fork and turn in the road, I would ask myself, "What would Jesus do if he were sitting right beside me?" Well, he is right beside you! If you have invited him into your heart, he will guide you like a river to the way he would have you go. We must learn to acknowledge him in all our ways, talk with him, and trust in him and thru our relationship with him, we shall prosper. Furthermore the Apostle Paul writes in Philippians 3:12-14:

"Not that I have already attained, or am already perfected; but I press on that I may lay hold of that for which Christ Jesus has also laid hold of me. Brethren, I do not count myself to have apprehended; but the one thing I do, forgetting those things which are behind and reaching forward to those things which are ahead, I press toward the goal for the prize of the upward call of God in Christ Jesus."

Paul teaches us in the passage that we must let go of those worldly things, which distract us from becoming like Christ. We must not focus on past mistakes and transgressions, nor should we be focused on the things of this world, which distract us from our upward call in Christ Jesus. Things such as finances, material things, and debt should not be pursued to the point where they become our focus. Paul is telling us that we must stay focused on the hope that God in Jesus Christ provides, and the faith that God can and will change us as we focus on knowing him better and serving him out of love, not duty.

The call to witness, the call to be pure in heart, the call to balance our lives between who we say we are in Christ and how we actually live out our daily lives is what we must witness to. Yes, Paul, too, was a sinner. He was no different from you or I, before he was saved. Paul tells Timothy of his past in the following passage,

1Timothy 1:13:

"Even though I was once a blasphemer and a persecutor and a violent man, I was shown mercy because I acted in ignorance and disbelief." (NIV)

28

God forgave Paul and he will forgive you, too. I am ashamed of my past, but I no longer regret it. God has forgiven me and I have forgiven myself. I am now trying to focus on how I can best serve God. God used Paul in an incredible way for the growth of his kingdom. I want God to use me as well. So, I ask, how about you? How can the experiences of your life benefit others once you are saved or now that you already are? The call to witness is purposeful, it is intentional, and we must let Jesus' light in us shine before men so that others may come to Christ!

In Ephesians, 4:1 Paul says it is time to change:

"As a prisoner for the Lord, then, I urge you to live a life worthy of the calling by which you have been called." (NIV)

Paul is commanding us to balance our lives between who we say we are in Christ and how we live. He is saying that it is not an option. It is the idea that we cannot be in Christ and not change. We must be growing and changing and striving daily to balance our lives. If we are not then are we truly living a life worthy of the calling we have received?

The calling I have received is to witness the miracle of transformation God has performed in my life. For close to five years now I have been meditating upon the Scripture and for that same period of time, the idea of witnessing and personal testimony has repeatedly jumped out of the text at me. I know that a big part of my transformation entails my testimony. Paul had an incredible gift for teaching the scriptures. Paul was steadfast in his duties and he endured all kinds of pain, physical and mental, to share the Gospel. Paul is telling us it is time to balance our lives; we are being called by Jesus Christ to live out the life that God has put in us.

In my life, the miracles God has bestowed upon me are numerous. God has chosen to save me from myself. In doing so God has healed me in the following ways:

- God removed the compulsive desire to drink alcoholically.
- God removed the compulsive desire to consume drugs even when death loomed imminent.
- God lifted the eating disorders, bleeding ulcers, and stomach problems that resided in me.
- God removed the deceitful desires of my heart.
- God stripped away the prideful vines that draped over my heart.
- God washed away my shame, guilt, and remorse for the person I had become.
- God said he loved me, even when I could not love myself.
- God gave me a new life in Christ Jesus.
- God gave me and continues to give me grace on a daily basis.
- The most important thing of all that I have received is the ability to look in the mirror and humbly respect the person that I am trying to be. God has given me "a spirit of self-worth."

Listen to what Paul tells us in 2 Timothy 1:7:

"For God did not give us a spirit of timidity, but a spirit of power, of love and of self-discipline." (NIV)

Yes, this is what God is calling me to do. This is what he wants me to say. This is how Jesus and I overcame my personal troubles. It is a miracle of transformation! It occurs on a daily basis and often when you do not realize it. God's sovereign grace guided me as the Holy Spirit and I did the footwork. God put the spirit of power, love, and self-discipline in my heart and he wants to do it for you.

OK, what does it mean to be called? Being called means that we have begun to know Jesus Christ, we have entered into a relationship with him, we are forgiven, we are justified, the seal of the Holy Spirit has been placed in us, and we are now living out of GRACE! Now we are being called to live our life in such a way that our beliefs match our behaviors. Hear the words of the Apostle John in John 1:6-9; (NIV)

"There came a man who was sent from God; his name was John. He came as a witness to testify concerning that light, so that thru him all men might believe. He himself was not the light; he came only as a witness to the light. The true light that gives light to every man was coming into the world."(NIV)

The Apostle John is telling us that John the Baptist was not the light and neither are we. Jesus Christ is the true light of the world and his followers, you and I, are called to reflect that light by leading others to Christ thru our witness and testimony of Gods work in our lives. We are to share how Jesus has changes our hearts, how we have become new creatures. We live so that whom we say we are in Christ we actually live out in our lives. Repeatedly in the scriptures, we hear Paul practicing what he preaches. The examples are limitless. Paul writes of the joy he has in Christ even when chains in prison have bound him for countless years. Yes, he had been stoned, chased out of towns, threatened, beaten, and whipped for his faith. Yet, Paul endured because his heart was for Jesus and his eye was on the prize. So where is your heart and where is God?

Through countless spiritual books, sermons, self-help groups, daily Bible study, and quiet time set aside with God for prayer, I have sought to grow my heart and spirituality. Through these activities, God has bestowed upon me many gifts. I hope you will read on and discover the wonderful works and

31

revelations God has provided in my life, and that you can find in your life.

In James 2:17, we read:

"In the same way, faith by itself, if not accompanied by action is dead." (NIV)

Here James, the brother of Jesus is telling us that even though we are saved by faith through grace we must still do good works. We serve God and perform good works because we understand who we are now. We are in Christ, justified, sins removed, grace bestowed. We do good deeds because we are motivated by love, not by a desire to win God's favor. We cannot win God's favor with deeds. The action we take is focused on knowing him better by meditating upon his word. The gift then becomes the manifestation of his word in our lives

Yes, I had to be beaten into submission. I had to be crushed. I had to be thoroughly convinced that of myself, I was nothing, but with complete and utter dependence on God, I could be made whole. Listen to the words of the Apostle John in John 15:5;

"I am the vine; you are the branches. If a man remains in me and I in him, he will bear much fruit, apart from me he can do nothing." (NIV)

In this scripture there are far to many ideas to grasp at this point. As we voyage deeper into developing a heart for Jesus, we will explore the ideas of the vine, the branches and bearing fruit. However, at this point, if we are committed to Christ then we are committed to the truth. The truth is the word of God and the word of God says, apart from Christ we can do nothing. Believe me, I tried for years, sure we can do the simple things like make money and get along, but Jesus is talking about living a truly productive lifestyle that reflects the image of God. Jesus is telling us that we will never be able to grasp the power of God and his grace in our lives until we completely give our hearts to him. God can and will restore you to wholeness, but first he must have all of you. I was completely beaten and I had nowhere else to turn. I learned that God was not interested in part of me. He knew when I had other roads planned, in case the God option did not work out. God was gracious enough to let me travel down every road I needed until I found the truth.

What is the truth, you might ask? This is what I intend to explore with you as we seek God's direction and guidance. By grace alone, I have walked from tears of pain and self-loathing to tears of joy, peace, and contentment. You, too, are made in the image of God and he is waiting for you to open your heart to him.

Jesus said, in Matthew 8:7-8:

"Ask, and it will be given to you; seek and you will find; knock, and the door will be opened to you. For everyone who asks receives, and he who seeks finds, and to him who knocks it will be opened."

I am a living witness to the truth of this Scripture. At the point in my life that I was finally beaten into submission, through the exercising of my own will. At the point at which I had no heart left. When I felt that life was no longer worth living, and I had resigned myself to the fact that even if there was a God he would not want anything to do with me, I had found true humility. I have heard humility defined as not thinking of myself less or not thinking less of myself, but not thinking of myself at all. For me, true humility came at the point when I realized that as a human, I had become a complete and utter failure. My utterly helpless and hopeless disposition at one point in my life gave rise to a most honest and sincere plea to

God for help, a prayer to relieve my heart of the burdens it could no longer carry. At this point, I was ready to submit my will and my life to God's care. It was an admission that I could no longer live my life on my own accord. The pain of not having a higher purpose in life, of which to commit myself to, was no longer bearable.

As I shared earlier when I was saved, when Jesus came into my heart, he filled me with his Holy Spirit and removed all guilt, sin, and shame from my heart. At that point, I knew that God was going to provide me with the strength, power and courage to rise above my past. Hear the words of Jesus in John 14:15-17;

"If you love me you will obey what I command. And I will ask the Father and he will give you another Counselor to be with you forever- the Spirit of truth. The world cannot accept him because it neither sees him nor knows him. But you know him, for he lives with you and will be in you." (NIV)

Wow, Jesus tells us that the Spirit of Truth will guide us, and we know Gods word is truth. Remember, in the beginning was the word, and the word was with God, and the word was God (John 1:1). OK, since Gods word is truth and we are living by truth now, are we not living in the Spirit? Because we are living in the Spirit, we are given the gift of the Holy Spirit as our guide. Over the years, I have reflected on this occurrence quite often. I have grown to learn and understand that my search in life was outward focused, where God is not. Coincidentally, what I was searching for was inside me all along. It was simple to understand now, all I had to do was open the door of my heart and welcome Jesus home, to the house of my heart. Revelation is a wonderful thing, however it comes only to those of us who rigorously pursue the knowledge of God, thru his word. As I continued in my hunger for understanding, I was learning that I must focus on protecting and growing my heart.

Why is your heart so important? Where does God reside? Let us seek him now!

Chapter 2 Study Guide
Q1: What miracles has God blessed you with?

Q2: Make a list of the things in your life that need to be balanced with the word of God.

Q3: DO you feel called? Please explain.

Q4: Are you completely ready and willing to accept Christ as your savior?

Q5: How do you plan to know God better? List your ideas and how you plan to schedule them!

Chapter 3

Where Is God?

It has been a couple of years since the horrible events
transpired at the World Trade Center. I cannot tell you how
many times I have heard the question, "Where is God?" Well, I
will tell you that I wanted to be able to answer that question so
badly it hurt! I wanted to be able to reach over to that person
that was struggling and fix their faith, but I did not have the
answer! Therefore, I began to seek the answer in scripture. As I
sought the answer through a daily practice of seeking the
knowledge of God through his word, I still could not quite put
my finger on the answer.

About a year ago, I was watching the movie We Were
Soldiers, in which Mel Gibson portrayed an army colonel in the
war with Vietnam. I remember the incredible feeling of sadness
and remorse I felt as I watched the true events of this story
unfold. I, too, found myself asking the question, "Where are you,
God?" "Where are you in events like this?" I felt a sense of
indignation rising up in me and as that indignation began to
grow, I felt separated from God.

Yes, at that crucial time in questioning the sovereign
power and grace of my creator, I began to realize the answer to
that question. It is about trust; it is about a heart for God. Do I
trust him only when things are good and discount him when
there are difficulties and trials? Do I trust the idea that all things
work together for good even though I cannot see that well,
because of the pain and destruction before me? I have come to
learn through meditation on Gods word that no matter how bad
things get in our lives, no matter how difficult things become,
our responsibility is clear. We are not to become discouraged,
but we are to remain faithful, always keeping the eyes of our
hearts focused on the hope that God in Christ Jesus provides. Let

us not focus on questioning our creator, but in fact, trusting in his word. Let us not focus on the speck in other people's behaviors, let us focus on the issues of our hearts. Let us not get caught up in the worldly issues but let us focus on the issues of the heart which lead us to the prize. In Romans 13:11-12, Paul tells us:

"And do this, understanding the present time. The hour has come for you to wake up from your slumber, because our salvation is nearer now than when we first believed. The night is nearly over; the day is almost here. So let us put aside deeds of darkness and put on the armor of light." (NIV)

In this scripture, Paul gets to the meat of our salvation. He is telling us that God is interested in the attitudes of our hearts. Dissension, envy, drunkenness, gossip, sexual immorality, your personal lusting when you are alone in your tent. We need to change these attitudes! These are the attitudes that keep us from God. When things turn bad in our lives, do we dispel the truth of the scriptures or do we hold fast to the promise? Do we turn to the very things that cause sin in our lives or do we cling to God and strive to keep our hearts pure? Paul tells us in 1 Corinthians 13:13:

"And now these three remain: faith, hope, and love. But the greatest of these is love." (NIV)

Faith, defined, is a complete trust and belief in the foundation and content of God's word and God's promise in Christ Jesus.

Hope, defined, is the attitude and the mind-set, it is the focus of my thinking, it is my heart's desire to believe in God the Father, God the Son, and God the Holy Spirit. It is only when my faith and my hope are aligned to the will of God that I am free to love and trust God completely.

As these scripture raced through my mind, I was finally able to quickly put things in perspective. I was quickly resolved to my faith. Yes, I finally had an answer to the question, "Where is God during the difficult times?" I can recall literally dozens of times lately when I have witnessed the pain of disease and hunger, the devastation of war, and the trials that soldiers must endure for their country, through the news. Watching the news can quickly become a painful and depressing stroll down the road of fear and doubt, where scenes of famine, disease, drought, war, and natural disaster are commonplace headlines. Be careful of what you allow to enter your heart and mind. If you let garbage in, it has to come out!

Are we drawn to the negativisms that pollute our minds and thread the very needle, which separates peace and chaos? Do we, as Christians, choose to focus on the chaos or do we focus on what is right, what is good, what is pure, what is Holy? The apostle Paul tells us in Philippians 4:4-9:

"Rejoice in the Lord always, I will say it again: Rejoice! Let your gentleness be evident to all. The Lord is near. Do not be anxious about anything, but in everything, by prayer and petition, with thanksgiving, present your requests to God. And the peace of God, which transcends all understanding, will guard your hearts and your minds in Christ Jesus. Finally, brothers, whatever is true, whatever is noble, whatever is right, whatever is pure, whatever is lovely, whatever is admirable — if anything is excellent or praiseworthy — think about such things. Whatever you have learned or received or heard from me, or seen in me — put into practice. And the God of peace will be with you." (NIV)

OK! Are you wondering why I keep putting scripture in front of you? Are you asking yourself what is the point and, "Where is God in these events?" The answer is so simple that you will gasp.

THE ANSWER: GOD IS WHEREVER YOU HAVE PLACED HIM.

If you question his sovereign grace and power, he will reside in your mind and you will always question him. If you choose to open up your heart to him, truly believe in the one God sent, let Jesus into your heart and give your heart, your mind, and your soul to him, he will dwell there.

Friends, this is where the true heart of transformation begins. At the point of total acceptance, we find a heart for Jesus. At the core of, A Hart for Jesus, we are bestowed the gifts of the Holy Spirit. We have reached the point in our journey where the desire to know God better brings peace, joy, direction, healing, and trust. At this point your hope, faith, and love are aligned with the will of God and your feet become securely fastened to the road ahead. This is absolute trust in the word of God, The Bible, the truth and the way. Folks we cannot subscribe to just parts of Bible. We absolutely must believe his entire word and live by Gods entire word. If God said it, I believe. We must relieve our intellect of the burden to understand God and his nature and some of his ways and reap the joy of absolute faith!

There was a time in my life when God was at church. As a child, going to church meant getting dressed up in nice clothes and sitting still for an hour to an hour and a half. At that point, in my life, I had no conception or understanding of who or what God was. Therefore, God was somewhere out there. For some reason, as a child I failed to make a connection between who God is and where he dwells. Today I spend a lot of time with my children talking about God, who he is, and where he lives. I tell my children that God lives in their hearts and that for them to know God they must pray and talk with him. We talk about the stories of the Bible and what they mean. We pray before meals and we pray on our knees in the morning and at night. We talk about the poor, the rich, the good and the bad. We try to teach our children from our experience that God is Love. That God loves mercy and kindness and that God's true will for us is to believe on his Son, love mercy, love justice, and walk humbly before him.

You see, it is imperative that we train ourselves as well as our children in the ways of God and where the spirit of God resides, and though we may lose our way, as we grow we will return to God.

I challenge you to pick up the Bible, turn to Proverbs, and count how many times the word "heart" appears. I have counted over seventy and that was speed flipping. Countless words of wisdom from King Solomon telling us to guard our hearts, train our hearts, and protect our hearts. Why is this so very important? It is a matter of the heart! I believe Jeremiah summed it up best when he says in Jeremiah 17:9:

"the Heart is deceitful above all things and beyond cure, who can understand it?" (NIV)

God is speaking through Jeremiah here and making it clear why we sin: "IT'S A MATTER OF THE HEART." Our hearts have been inclined towards sin since the day we were born. Why is this so, you may ask? To understand the answer to this question we must go back to the Old Testament to understand why our hearts are inclined towards sin. In Genesis 3, we read of the fall of man. Before we enter this dialogue, you must have the understanding that before Adam and Eve, there was a great rebellion in the heavens. God expelled Satan from heaven and he came to dwell on Earth. Satan's sole purpose is to tempt us to walk away from God. The serpent that is described is Satan and Satan came for the sole purpose of tempting Eve. Satan tempted Eve with what has become the timeless fall of mankind. It is the prideful idea that we can be all powerful and all knowing. It is the idea that we can rule over others. Satan tempted Eve with the idea that she could be like God, little did she understand that she was made in the image of God. Satan told Eve that God did not want her to eat of the forbidden fruit because then she would be equal to God and have the same power of the knowledge of good and evil. Yes, Eve bought into the deception of Satan, and guess what, Adam was right there beside her the whole time. What did he do? Not a thing, he did not even lift his voice in disapproval. The Scripture says in Genesis 3:6,

"...she took some and ate it. She also gave some to her husband, who was with her, and he ate it." (NIV)

Herein lies the truth about sin. It is a matter of the heart! This was the beginning of sin in man! Eve's heart's desire was to eat of the apple because it would make her more powerful, so she thought, even when she knew God had forbade it. Did Adam and Eve have a heart for God? Sure, I would say they did. They also had a greater heart for power and the knowledge that the tree offered. At that critical point in the timeline of mankind, Adam and Eve chose personal advancement, they chose personal pride, the kind of pride that says my ways are better than God's ways and in so doing endeared mankind to a sinful, deceitful, and prideful heart.

So, why do you believe it is so important to protect our hearts? Lets look a bit further into Eve's reply to the serpent in Genesis 3:3;

"But God did say, you must not eat fruit from the tree that is in the middle of the garden and you must not touch it or you will die." (NIV)

Do you hear the words Eve uses? She said God not only said do not eat the fruit but that we also should not touch it! Why do you think God cautioned Eve not to touch the fruit?

41

First of all, God did not say, "do not touch it," Eve said this. Why do you think Eve said God said this. I believe God and Eve had a more extensive conversation than what The Bible possibly reveals. I believe God may have warned Eve of the dangers of touching something that is forbidden. I believe God is trying to teach Eve and us about temptation. What happens to you when you start lusting for something? The first thing that happens is; the thing you lust for appears in your thinking or your thought life, then if you reach out for that thing and touch it or you roll that thought around in your head for a while, what happens? If you touch it, are you more likely to put it down or act on it? I believe we are more likely to act on it. When we lust, then we touch, we usually act on the lustful thought, however if when we lust and we chose not to touch and turn to God, we invoke the power he has placed in us to resist the devil or temptation. Are you hearing this? God said we should not eat of the fruit! Eve added , that we should not touch it either. Folks, this is wonderful wisdom, it is a warning to us that once we act on our thoughts we have passed the point of resisting temptation. So, keep your hands off the fruit, or the car or the married person or whatever it is that does not agree with the word of God!

Let us go one step further and we can understand fear as well. Not too long after they ate of the forbidden fruit did they realize that they were naked. They sewed fig leaves together to cover themselves. Then they heard God walking in the garden and God called out to Adam in Genesis 3:9:
"But the Lord God called to the man, "Where are You?"(NIV)

Adam's response in Genesis 3:10 was:

"… I heard you in the Garden and I was AFRAID because I was naked, so I hid." (NIV)

Moreover, fear was ushered into mankind. You see, Adam and Eve became fearful of God because they did not obey

42

God. This opened the door to all types of fear for mankind. The fear of failure, the fear of death, the fear of being found out and the list continues. Adam did many things for mankind; he is actually the father of the human race. He was the first human to share an intimate relationship with God. He was, by trade, the first gardener. He actually named the animals. Adam's impact on man was far greater than any work he could have done. Adam sat by and watched Eve disobey God's command. Therefore, he and Eve together brought a heart for sin into this world. Adam and Eve also brought fear into our lives by eating the apple. However, wait a minute, he did not stop there. He actually blamed Eve for giving him the apple. What is this called today? I would call it not accepting responsibility for our actions. It is called passing the buck, shifting the responsibility! Look at the speck in someone else's eye when there is a log in your own. In Genesis 3:11-12 we hear the dialogue between Adam and God;

"And God said, who told you that you were naked? Have you eaten from the tree that I commanded you not to eat from? Adam said, The woman you put here with me — she gave me some fruit from the tree, and I ate it."

Wait a minute, what just happened here? Adam actually placed blame on Eve's shoulders for what he did. Since the beginning of time, we see man's heart as deceitful and unwilling to accept responsibility for his actions. I believe it is a matter of the heart! You see, finding fault with others seems to alleviate us of the scriptural duty to remove the log from our own eye. Therefore, what happened after that? In Genesis 3:22, we see the final and painful consequences of their actions. God says:
"And the Lord God said, the man has now become like one of us, knowing good and evil. He must not be allowed to reach out his hand and take also from the tree of life and eat, and live forever." (NIV)

So there it is, our destiny revealed to us. We are born with a heart for sin; we are born destined to return to the dust from which we were created. What an incredible story about the fall of mankind. An understanding of what God intended us to be and what we truly are.

This is the truth! This is the root of the problem! This is our nature! As humans, we are born with a sinful heart. As we have mentioned, in order for transformation to take place in our lives, change must be rooted in the truth. You see, before we can experience the fruit of the truth we must understand the root of the truth.

For many years, I believed that I was far too sinful for God to want anything to do with me. The problem was a lack of understanding, or spiritual ignorance. I did not understand where God was or where he dwelled. More importantly, I did not realize who I was in Christ, and who I was by my first birthright. First, we are born of Adam, we are born of the earth and to the earth, we shall return. However, when we are saved, when we are made alive in Christ, we are born again of the spirit. We are a new creation. Sure, our bodies will still return to the earth from which it came, but our spirits will live forever in paradise!

OK, some of you are probably saying, this guy is a crackpot, there is no way God created him to become an alcoholic. Maybe not! What I am saying, though, is that God created me to have the freedom of choice. God gave me the choice, or the freedom, to follow him or my own personal sinful desires that arise out of my own heart. My sinful nature was inherited from Adam in the Garden of Eden. Understanding this gives me the power to discern the difference between being born of the flesh with a deceitful heart and being born again into Christ's family where my purpose becomes sanctification and my goal is the eternal crown. Sanctification, being the process of crucifying the sinful desires of my heart and becoming like Christ.

OK, are you hearing me? Are you beginning to understand who you are? Now, what do we do about it? How do we balance our lives between who we say we are in Christ and how we actually live out our lives on a daily basis? Listen, anyone can claim Christ! I see people every day wearing crosses or crucifixes that gives the impression that they trust Jesus and they are saved. With that representation, they are using foul language and living in drunkenness and/or sexual immorality. I see people with fish emblems on their vehicles flipping people off in traffic. I hear athletes, claiming God as the reason for their success that end up with drug, guns, and other criminal charges. We are seeing ministers and priests being arrested for criminal sexual behaviors. I am not picking on anyone here; Lord knows I have my share of sins.

What we must understand here is that when we claim Christ, when we ask him into our lives, this is only the beginning. Jesus did not die for our sins to justify or make us right with God, so we can return to our old ways. We cannot ask for forgiveness and hold on to the faulty idea that we can keep sinning because we will be forgiven. Neither can we create a long list of rules and regulations that dictate a code of morality that says we must do these things for God to love us. No, the proof is not in what we say about how we live our lives but is rooted in how we actually live out who we say we are in Christ. The very idea that we can say we are in Christ but refuse to grow and change the behaviors that do not agree with the word of God is a complete falsehood. We must strive to remove the things from our hearts that cause us to sin.

Once we have accepted Christ into our hearts and we are saved, we must begin our walk of faith. Once the gift of the Holy

Spirit is placed in your heart you must follow the advice of Solomon in Proverbs 3:5:

"Trust in the Lord with all your heart and lean not unto your own understanding, in all your ways acknowledge him and he will make straight your paths." (NIV)

I do not know about you, but I get the idea that Solomon is telling us to lean on God; it is the sense of complete rest in God that he will keep his promise. It is the idea that we must not be wise in our own eyes and that we must always be willing to listen to and heed the way and will of God. Solomon is telling us that if we want to receive the gift of God's guidance we must turn over all of our ways to him. God does not want just some of you. He wants all of you! Remember, in all we do, we must agree with God, his word, to live by the spirit. What are your values, what are you struggling with, what keeps you from grace? Do you need to open some closet doors in your life? Do you want the keys to open those doors? I know I do and the only way to find the right key is to meditate on God's word. You must work at knowing him better.

Uh oh, did I say work! Yes, I did. At the heart of American culture, and I know because I have lived it, is a faulty desire! This desire or goal is similar to Adam's and Eve's, a heart's desire to get more, to do more, to have more, to win at life on Earth, to succeed, prosperity is the end all be all, my peers will look up to me, my fellow man will bow down to me, and my castle will be my reward. In this culture, we have placed God in the same place Adam and Eve did. We have put him in the passenger seat. We have mistaken Christianity as a way to be prosperous; we have made Christianity into how to have a nice car, a nice home, healthy kids, and a happy marriage. We have turned Christianity into the idea that as long as we do good deeds God will love us. As long as I go to church fairly often, tithe a little bit, and do a little service work, I will be OK in God's eyes. These things are fine, but we must stop and ask ourselves, if this is our ideal, where have we placed God. Have we placed God in our hearts and are we living for him or have we placed God in the passenger seat, using him to get what we think we want in life?

So I ask you, where is God in your life? In what areas of your life is God driving and in what areas is he a passenger? What does it look like to balance your life between who you say you are in Christ and how you live?

Chapter 3 Study Guide

Q1: How do worldly events affect you and your understanding of God?

Q2: Write about faith, love and hope. Share your experiences and how the scripture may have helped you to adjust your perspective.

Q3: Where does God reside in your life?

Q4: How do you feel about Jeremiah's words about the heart?

Q5: How do you feel about your heart?

Q6: How are you tempted?

Q7: What are you fearful about?

Q8: Do you have any logs in your eyes and how do they relate to your problems with other people?

Chapter 4
Balancing our Lives

I would submit to you that the areas in your life where you are struggling the most are the ones you are not prepared to give to God. Why have you not completely given them to God? Right now, I am struggling with financial fear and the fear of writing this book. Even though I know God is calling me to share, Satan is telling me I will lose everything when people find out who I really am. So what do I do? I trust that God is sovereign and I press on, toward the mark, for my upward call in Christ Jesus. I press on not because I have a feeling of debt towards Christ for what he did for me, but because I love him for what he did for me! In Ephesians 3:16-19, Paul actually tells us where Christ's Spirit dwells:

"I pray that out of his glorious riches he may strengthen you with power through his Spirit in your inner being, so that Christ may dwell in your hearts through faith. And I pray that you being rooted and established in love, may have power, together with all the saints, to grasp how wide and long and high and deep is the love of Christ, and to know this love that surpasses knowledge — that you may be filled to the measure of all the fullness of God." (NIV)

Here, Paul explains to us where Christ dwells when we are one with the Father, Son, and Holy Spirit. The Holy Spirit dwells in our inner being, our hearts, and that by remaining faithful to our calling, Christ will dwell in our hearts and we will become rooted and established in love. There is that word, root, again. Why do you think we keep hearing that word? I believe it is intentional. What does it say in John 17:17:

"Sanctify them by the truth, your word is truth." (NIV)

Are you getting the picture? God's word is the truth! So, Gods word is truth and God the Father, God the Son and God the Holy Spirit are one, then if we want to live by the spirit if we want to develop a heart for Jesus we must live by Gods word. OK, we understand the truth is God's word. We also understand that our truth is that we were born with a sinful nature because we were born of Adam. Now that we understand the root of our heritage, we can see the fruit of the promise. We have the promise of transformation in the resurrection of Jesus Christ. We have the promise of a powerful new life and the promise of eternal life. He also tells us that together with all the saints we must grasp the power of God's love and begin to understand that his love surpasses all knowledge. Paul uses the word together that is to say that we cannot do it alone. In fact, we see the word, together, quite often. Paul is trying to give us a glimpse of the body of Christ. Together with the saints represents the idea that there is a Church, or group of Christians, loving, serving, building one another up, and growing together in their faith. He portrays the idea that we need others to grow. He says that we may have the power together with all the saints. He goes on to tell us that he wants us to know this love, so that we may know the "fullness of Christ." He is saying that only in Christ and through Christ's empowering spirit are we complete. In other words, for us to understand and know the fullness of Christ, Christ must reside in your heart. Paul is telling us that all of God was in Christ's human body. When Christ resides in our hearts, we have everything we need for salvation and right living. Having a Heart for Jesus, allows Christ the opportunity to live out the remainder of his life through us. He dwells in our hearts, he is the unique source of grace, wisdom, power, and knowledge from which we must live. In Colossians 2:9-12, Paul carries the idea a bit further. He says:

"For in Christ all the fullness of the Deity lives in bodily form and you have been given the fullness in Christ, who is the head over every power and authority. In him you were also circumcised, in putting off the sinful nature, not with a circumcision done with the hands of men but with the circumcision done by Christ, having been buried with him in baptism and raised in him through your faith in the power of God, who raised him from the dead." (NIV)

The idea Paul is portraying here is that we have had a spiritual circumcision, so to speak. In the Old Testament times, circumcision was the sign of the Jewish covenant with God. However, with Christ's work on the Cross, circumcision was not needed anymore. Now our commitment to God has been written on our hearts. Christ sets our hearts free from their evil desires by a spiritual operation, not a physical one. In this operation, God removes the old nature from our hearts and gives us a new nature.

So what does Paul mean when he says we were buried with him in baptism. He is trying to tell us that when we are baptized we are signifying the death and burial of our old sinful ways. It draws a parallel to the death, burial, and resurrection of Christ Jesus, and places us together with Jesus as he died for the sin of the world, so in the same manner our old natures are buried with him and our new natures are resurrected with Jesus Christ when we invite Christ into our hearts. This is why we immediately begin the process of transformation, we cannot wait, it is time to change, and we are called to let Jesus live out his life through us.

Do you understand the magnitude of what Paul is telling us here? Do you get it? We cannot invite Christ into our hearts, go through the process of baptism with him, be resurrected to our new lives with him, then stiff-arm change. The very idea that we may take baptism lightly or that we do not understand the magnitude of what is at stake when we fail to balance our lives between who we say we are in Christ and how we live each day is perilous.

Why, you might ask? I will tell you exactly why! Think about the world today. The world is trying to get God out of our schools, our government; crime is off the charts; and sin is rampant. Our culture and our morals in this country are lower than they have ever been. We have sexual misconduct running rampant in the Catholic Church. We have an openly gay bishop that has been confirmed by the Church. Why are these things happening?

I believe the answer lies in the complete lack of understanding about who we are in Christ. Let us look at the openly gay bishop, for example only. Now I want to first tell you that the man is probably a wonderful man and I do not in any way claim to have any superiority or inferiority in relation to him. He is a Brother in Christ. Regrettably, he is a shining example of our seeming inability to balance our lives! The reason I choose this example is that it poignantly identifies the root cause of our failure as humans to transform our lives. This man is openly gay and openly defying God's written law. However, our church recognizes him as a leader. Here is the problem! If I am in Christ, if I am saved, and if I am truly seeking to be Christ like, if I am truly in the word, then I am practicing Ephesians 4:20-24; where Paul says:

"You, however, did not come to know Christ in that way. Surely you heard of him and were taught in him in accordance with the truth that is in Jesus. You were taught with your former way of life, to put off your old self which is being corrupted by its deceitful desires, to be made new in the attitudes of your mind; and to put on the new self, created to be like God in true righteousness and holiness." (NIV)

What is Paul teaching us here? The scripture is teaching us that transformation, growth, and change require the daily practice of crucifying the flesh. Putting off those sinful desires

51

that contradict what God made us to be. Remember, sin is the disparity between who we are and who we are created to be. We then must focus on renewing the attitudes of our hearts and minds by putting a stop to acting on impulsive decisions and actions that are prompted by the body. We should focus on the prize instead of worry. We must change the way we think because we are a new creation now.

Now we are focusing on the things of God by meditating on his word. We are now living a new life that is led by the Holy Spirit. Now, when thoughts, feelings, and desires arise that are contrary to our new nature, we at once ask God to remove them. If temptation dogs us at every turn, we cry out to God for relief. When we are saved and we become justified in Christ, then we begin the process of sanctification. Sanctification is the process of balancing the scales. It is a lifelong process. In Colossians 1:10-14 Paul says:

"And we pray that you may live a life worthy of the Lord and may please him in every way; bearing fruit in every good work, growing in the knowledge of God, being strengthened with all power according to his glorious might so that you may have great endurance and patience and joyfully giving thanks to the Father, who had qualified you, to share in the inheritance of the saints in the kingdom of light. For he has rescued us from the dominion of darkness and brought us into the kingdom of the Son he loves, in whom we have redemption, the forgiveness of sins."

Did you really read this? If so, have you meditated upon it? If you have gathered this information and practiced meditation on it, then you should begin to receive the power of revelation. The power of this scripture is the truth of who we were when we lived in darkness, who we are now as Christians, and the process by which we are called to balance our lives. Paul uses the phrase, "that you may live a life worthy of the Lord" also, in Ephesians 4:1; again we hear Paul command us when he says:

"As a prisoner for the Lord, then, I urge you to live a life worthy of the calling you have received."

The phrases "worthy of the calling" and " that you may live a life worthy of the Lord" give us the picture of balancing our lives. Worthy means to be equal to our calling to do no less than our Father in Heaven would do.

OK, so how does this relate to the gay bishop? Let me draw the parallel. If he is truly a Christian, then he has the freedom to choose transformation by practicing Ephesians 4:20-24, and he is openly committed to crucifying the sinful desires and acts of homosexuality. Is this man truly trying to be Christ like or has he chosen to stiff-arm God in this one area? This man is probably of much greater stature than most of us in his knowledge of God, Scripture, and in all areas of theology; however, if he has chosen to disobey God's word in this one area then what is he saying about God? He is saying, "God, you are going to be this kind of God to me and I am going to mold you into the God I want you to be. Therefore, I am comfortable and I will still be saved."

The bishop is saying that it is OK to defy God in one area of your life as long as you follow his word in the other areas of your life. He is setting the bar, the benchmark, if you will, for all those who want to know what this God thing is all about and he is sending the wrong message! What is he saying, you may ask. He is telling any Christian who does not understand who he is in Christ or any other person who is seeking or wondering about Christ that it is ok to manipulate God's word. It is ok to create the kind of God that works for you! Herein lies the enormity of what is at stake when we twist scripture to fit our own idea of who God is. In Ephesians 4:4-6 Paul says:

"There is one body and one spirit—just as you were called to one hope when you were called—one Lord, one faith, one baptism; one God and Father of all, who is over all in all and through all." (NIV)

What Paul is telling us is that all believers in Christ are united in one body and we are under one head of the Church, Christ himself. Paul goes on to say that God is over all, in all, and through all. This means that God transcends all things, he is actively present in all our lives as believers and unites us as one under Christ Jesus and his imminence reigns supreme. Regrettably, the message we get as Christians when a gay bishop is confirmed in the Church is that it is ok to redefine God, his word, the truth. The bishop is telling us that there is not one Body, not one Lord, not one Father, not one baptism! Can you see the problem here? The Bishop is telling us, by his actions, there is another God out there that approves of men lying with other men. For further understanding, I suggest studying Paul's first letter to the Church of Corinth. How can we say we believe in God, but we do not believe his word on homosexuality? We cannot! Is it ok for a married man to lay with another woman? Of course not! Why is it OK to defy Gods written word (i.e the Church confirms gay pastors), but it is not OK to defy mans written law (the church denounces sexual sin from pastors or priests)? So why is it ok to redefine God with homosexuality? I believe it is because the church has lost its heart for Jesus. The church is so afraid it is going to hurt someone that they do not recall how to speak the truth in love and stand by the word of God. Well, you may be saving a few but your leading flocks of sheep astray in the process! People, there is no grey area here; if we fall in one area we fall in all areas, sin is sin, the message is the message and our choices are our choices. The Lord said wide is the gate and narrow is the door that leads to salvation. Why? We make our own choice to follow the will and way of God or the will of our flesh. We are made in the image of God, God prompts us to come to him through the Holy Spirit, but ultimately the choice to come to Jesus is ours. Leaders in Gods church are charged with the duty of leading their flock to salvation not slaughter.

However you choose to view this, it is only a piece in the puzzle. What we are hearing and seeing from the gay bishop is no different from me when I say I am in Christ and I act on my sinful nature, without remorse or repentance. The issue is not whether he is gay, whether you killed a man, whether I lusted today, or whether or not one of you stole, lied, or cheated this morning. We do, we did, and we probably will again! The issue is: IF YOU ARE, IN CHRIST, THEN YOU ARE LIVING OUT OF THE PRINCIPLES IN EPHESIANS 4:20-24. IF YOU ARE NOT REPENTING OF YOUR SIN AND PUTTING ON THE NEW, THEN YOU ARE NOT PRACTICING THE PROCESS OF SANCTIFICATION.

Men and women in positions of leadership in the Church must have, as their ultimate priority, balancing their lives between who they say they are in Christ and how they live their lives. As far as I am concerned the gay bishop is telling everyone it is OK to live in sin, it is OK to commit adultery, kill, steal, lie, cheat, covet, lust worship idols, whatever your preference is as long as you try to live out the rest of your life trying to be a Christian. He or anyone who is in Christ and subscribes to this idea is perverting the idea of Spiritual Transformation. This type of thinking is demeaning the temple of God. It is saying that my will and my ways are better than God's. As a leader in the Church, this man is projecting his unwilling penitence and his willful disobedience of God's command, just like Adam and Eve did in the Garden of Eden.

Well, we have already seen the results of man's defiance of God's word in the Garden of Eden. Dare I presume the outcome here!

OK, enough of this! I pray for this bishop and hope that God will open the eyes of his heart in this area of his life; AND THAT God will open the eyes of my heart if I am sinning against him in a way in which I cannot see. Every day my flesh wants to do sinful things. Every day my flesh wills me to lust or do something that is sinful, but as I am committed to Christ and to the discipline of transformation, I must not act on that earthly desire. Let me say that I fail, but true to Ephesians, I get up and strive to put off the old, renew my mind, and put on the new. As a leader in any church, those persons must be leading the charge in the area of spiritual transformation.

The process of sanctification is grounded in crucifying our sinful nature. Our sinful nature is our flesh. Why do I keep saying our flesh wants to do sinful things? What really is the flesh? Our flesh is OUR way of thinking. Our flesh is OUR thought life that does not agree with the word of God. We were born of the first Adam with a sinful nature. This sinful nature is not your loins or the actual skin on your body; our sinful nature or our flesh is a way of thinking. Just as Gods word is truth and we live by Gods word then we are living in the spirit and to the contrary if we are living in deeds, thoughts and actions that are contrary to Gods word or are against what God teaches us then we are living in the flesh. In other words, if our thought life is based on our desires, which do not agree with the word of God, then we are living in the flesh.

Brothers and Sisters in Christ, we have to stop and ask ourselves what is at stake here. I can name handfuls of people who are not attending church because leadership does not reflect Christian values. If Christ is the way and the life, why do the Church's actions not reflect its values? Why do individual leaders in the church act on self instead of preserving the unity of the Spirit? I submit that the answer lies in the lack of understanding of who we are in Christ and how we crucify our flesh. It is a lack of knowledge, which comes from seeking the things of this world instead of the word of God. Do the members of the Church understand the magnitude of their call to balance their lives between their actions and Christian values? Let us look at how Paul balanced his life between his old sinful nature and his new nature in Christ. In Romans 7:14-23:

"We know that the law is spiritual; but I am unspiritual, sold as a slave to sin. I do not understand what I do. For what I want to do I do not do, but what I hate I do. For if I do what I do not want to do, I agree the law is good. As it is no longer I myself who do it, but it is sin living in me. I know that nothing good lives in me, that is, in my sinful nature. For I have the desire to do what is good, but I cannot carry it out. For what I do is not the good I want to do; no, the evil I do not want to do — this I keep doing. Now if I do what I do not want to do, it is no longer I who do it, but it is sin living in me that does it. So I find this law at work: When I want to do good, evil is right there with me. For in my inner being I delight in God's law; but I see another law at work in the members of my body, waging war against the law of my mind and making me a prisoner of the law of sin at work in my members." (NIV)

I invite you to read and reread that passage. Chew on it until you are able to understand what Paul is saying here. This passage for me sums up the meat of the sanctification process. Therefore, we must chew on it until we can completely absorb the depth of the journey we are traveling. Paul is telling us that even though we are a new person in Christ we still have two natures. Remember, we were born of Adam in the Garden of Eden, and in that birth, we received a sinful nature or a heart for sin. When we are saved, we are now in Christ, we have a new nature, we have a heart for Jesus, and we are justified. We have imputed righteousness and grace.

Even though we have righteousness in God's eyes, we still possess the old sinful nature, complete with its evil desires. What we have encountered is the eternal struggle of man. It is the clash between his two natures. One nature is born of Adam and the other being born of the Spirit. What Paul is telling us is now that we have a heart for Jesus and we want to do well, our bodies still have their sinful desires. The members of our bodies still seek the things of this world while our hearts crave a life of righteousness. While the battle rages between our hearts and our bodies the law should be used as a guide to show us where we are going astray and it will help us to realize that if we are trying to defeat the sin in our body of our own strength, then we have already slipped into sins grasp. Paul shares three lessons that will help us understand how to deal with our old sinful desires. He suggests that:

1. We do not seek knowledge to overcome our sinful desires.
2. We do not try to have success over our sinful desires through self-determination.
3. We must realize that even though we are saved we were never promised that the desire to sin and temptation would not be a part of our lives.

Great, then how do we deal with temptation? We must change the way we think about God and sin. When we desire to sin we do not try to run from it, we turn to the word of God, we pray for courage to turn and we focus on Gods word, which is truth!

Personal Testimony about Temptation

Early on in my recovery, I learned that temptation would strike and sometimes it would strike painfully hard and without warning. I learned how to prepare myself for temptation by following some simple rules.

God will help me overcome temptation by:

- Recognizing familiar people, habits, places, and activities that give me trouble and stay away from them.
- Turning away from anything that we know is wrong. We must be rigorously honest here.
- Choose to do only those things that are right.
- Always, without ceasing, cry out to God for help.
- Finally, surround yourself with friends who love God as you do and can offer help when you are tempted.

When I was living in my addictions, my cravings surpassed all things and I would act on them. Believe me, once I was saved, these cravings did not just disappear. I had to train my body to understand them and then pray them away. I had to train my mind to change the way I thought. I had to think on Godly things not fleshly desires. I learned that just because my body is telling me something does not mean that it is true or that I have to act on it. I was taught that it is not the sinful thought that occurs in my mind that I am responsible for. That is my old nature! How I respond to that thought is what I am responsible for. This response is my new nature, the spirit of power and self-discipline, guided by the Holy Spirit who dwells within my heart.

There were many times when I dreadfully wanted to fall back into my old ways. Some days I wanted to run and use so badly I thought I would die. You see, I began to realize through training my body that I did not want to feel the pain, nor had I ever wanted to feel any of life's emotions. For some reason, I did not have the moral capacity to deal with human emotions so I covered them up with alcohol and drugs.

The victory for me was that each time I followed the instructions given to me, the cravings got less intense and fewer and farther in between, and getting through got easier. It was the principle of Godly discipline that I was not aware of until many years later that worked so well in my life. Then at some point in that first ninety days after my treatment, I woke up and thought, "You know what, I have not had those cravings in a long time." I do remember this, for over ten years I was driven by the phenomenon of craving and somewhere in the later part of those first ninety days, the miracle occurred. Through the process of self-discipline, God reached inside of me and cured that craving, that insidious desire to self-destruct. It taught me a valuable lesson. God loves me and desires to make me whole. He wants to save me from my destructive ways. I began to learn that the road to holiness is about God making me whole from the inside out! In 1 Corinthians 10:13 Paul says:

"No temptation has seized you except what is common to man. And God is Faithful, he will not let you be tempted beyond what you can bear, but when you are tempted he will also provide you a way out so that you can stand up under it." (NIV)

In essence, what Paul is saying is that in his time his culture was filled with sin-inducing worldly pressures and shrouded in moral ambiguity. In fact, quite often, the fog is so dangerously thick, that we are tempted to say, "Who will know? Doesn't everyone do it?" Paul says that even in his day, these temptations were rampant and we should not feel singled out because we are human and we all have these temptations in our lives. The difference between a Christian and another is how we react to these temptations. Paul says that many before us have resisted and with the guidance of the Holy Spirit, we can, too. We must cling to God and keep our eyes on the prize and how we can serve.

So how do we overcome our sinful nature? First, we must be committed to our faith and our new walk in life. We must go into training. However, before we go into training let us take a closer look at our nature in Christ.

60

Chapter 4 Study Guide

Q1: What areas of your life are you struggling to balance?

Q2: Explain your perception of the Holy Spirit and where he dwells.

Q3: Do you have knowledge of the Holy Spirit and how he can help you? Please explain.

Q4: Talk about your sinful nature and your new nature. How do they war against one another and what are you doing about it?

Q5: Share your concerns, roadblocks and frustrations with our church culture today. How can we change things?

Q6: Are you so comfortable with a few sins in your life that you are not willing to give them up?

Q7: Are you ready for the process of Godly sanctification? Explain what you need to do.

Chapter 5

Our True character in Christ

Ezekiel 36:26

"I will give you a new heart and put a new spirit in you;" (NIV)

Proverbs 3:5-6

"Trust in the Lord with all your heart and lean not on your own understanding; in all your ways acknowledge him and he will make your paths straight." (NIV)

Do any of you need your paths straightened? I know I do! Solomon is giving us Godly wisdom about how we should live. He is telling us that we should trust God with all our hearts and not try to understand God with our minds. Knowledge of God and his ways surpasses our ability to comprehend and can only bring us frustration.

Following is an interview I heard. A successful individual was asked the question, "What do you attribute your enormous success to?" He said, "I could sum that up in two words, 'good decisions.'" Then he was asked, "How were you able to make such good decisions?" He responded, "I can sum that up in one word, 'experience.'" A bit bewildered, the person asking the questions pondered a moment and then responded, "How did you gain all this experience?" The man responded, "I can sum that up in two words, 'bad decisions.'"

I do not know about you, but I certainly resemble those remarks. I have spent the better part of my life making bad decisions that were based on self. I have learned that I must first choose God and then ensure that my decisions agree with sound Godly wisdom that is provided to us in The Bible. A hard concept for many of us to grasp is aligning our will with the will of God. To make decisions that will be Christ motivated, in order to better his kingdom, and God centered, instead of self centered.

As we begin the process of transformation, as we begin our new walk, I believe it is imperative that we understand our nature in Christ, so that when those daily choices present themselves we will be equipped to make good decisions.

Personal Testimony about Choices

In my first few years of marriage, my wife and I never really knew how to communicate. Oh yes, we loved each other, but we did not know how to communicate. Things would get stressful, money was tight, the kids were screaming, we would get in a fight. We would not talk for a day or two and finally one of us would finally give in and say, "I am sorry," and we would kiss and make up. We would never actually address the root of the problem.

The root of the problem was that neither one of us was willing to hear what the other one had to say, we both wanted to be heard so badly, to be right, to have our feelings acknowledged, that we fought to the point of painful separation, only to reconcile out of a desire not to hurt anymore. After numerous conflicts, we made a conscious decision or choice to try to work on it together. The gift of that decision was that God did help us find our way together. The Sovereign gardener pruned my pride enough to get me to agree to go to a marriage counselor. You see, for me agreeing to go get help was an admission of failure, and I had already failed at life enough. By admitting that I needed help, by making a God-centered decision, or agreeing with what God says, instead of a self-centered decision, and agreeing with my thinking or what my flesh says, I have been empowered to live a much more joyful and fulfilling life.

We must be ever mindful of Satan's power and presence in this world. He will be at work in our lives, working on our pride all the time, when we least expect it. I wanted to be able to do it on my own, and that in itself was and still can be my number one downfall. My pride, the kind of pride that says my ways, my thoughts, and my beliefs are more important than yours or Gods.

This is why pride is so sinful and so insidious, it invades our heart without our knowledge and, if unchecked, it comes out in our relationships. My sinful pride was, and still is if not daily kept in check, the kind of pride that says my ideas, my thoughts, my needs, my dreams, my ways are more important than yours or Gods. It is the I-know-best-and-I-can-do-it-better, self-reliant kind of pride that separates me from the sunlight of the spirit and isolates me from the Christian community. This is my number one offender, my most poignant character defect.

So God's way was to break my pride. This came in the courage of a command from my wife that we would go to a counselor or else. Well, I did not want to know what the else was. You see, I loved her dearly but I did not know how to communicate with her, nor did I understand her emotions.

A little more background about our relationship:

You see, after we had been married for a few years, she went through a very difficult time with her second pregnancy. She was carrying twins and she lost them after close to six months. The doctor said they became tangled around each other's umbilical cords and suffocated. Paige was deeply saddened and I did not know how to handle it. I stuffed it and could not understand why she could not get past it. It came out

64

of me in the form of anger and walls that I could not figure out. She tried to work through it with me, but I was unavailable. Well I knew I had no choice but to choose to go get counseling. So off, we went to all types of marriage and child loss counseling. We made a choice to endure, especially me. I was the one who had all the male communication brain damage! We endured many trips to the marriage counselor that caused great frustration, extraordinary pain, and finally a life-changing result that gave us the freedom to communicate.

You see, we both had issues and neither one of us was good at communicating. The counselor realized this and pointed out my anger and the walls I erected in my confrontations with my wife. The counselor also pointed out that the way my wife fought was unfair, too. She kept digging up every little thing I had ever done wrong. The counselor taught us to put our anger and our frustration on neutral ground by using, "I feel" and "I hear" messages, and agreeing to allow the other to speak until he or she was finished. Then she suggested that we should calmly repeat what we heard the other one say by beginning with, "OK, so what I hear you saying is that I hurt you and you feel like I am going to leave you when I get angry, scream at you, then put up a wall, and do not communicate with you." She says, "Yes." Then I understand her because I hear what is hurting her and I am no longer blocked by what I want. This became a new beginning for us, a true gift of how to listen to one another. More to the point though, it taught me that in order to listen to anyone, especially God, I must take the thick heavy cotton of pride out of my ears, put it in my mouth, and listen. It taught me that I must make God- centered decisions and not self-centered decisions. So before you act or walk through the choice you are about to make, ask Jesus what he would do if he were sitting right there with you. Play it out in your heart and, above all, use Christ as your guide.

So how does God view us? What do we look like to God? What happens to all the sins we have committed before we where saved? What happens if I sin after I have been saved? In my conversations with others, I have found that many do not understand God and where we stand in his eyes. It seems as though most of us do not understand how God views us. This can lead all of us down a road of misunderstanding and frustration that can ultimately cause us to walk away from God because we cannot quit sinning. Let us take a walk through some theological terms that will give us a better understanding of how God sees us when we come to him through faith in Jesus Christ.

Election

For me, I must ask why would God choose to save a sinner like me. The best answer can be found in Genesis 1:27;

"So God created man in his own image, in the image of God he created him; male and female he created them."(NIV)

This is more than sufficient for me. God said it! He created us in his own image and likeness. Thus, there is the theological doctrine of Election where Paul says that no one can claim to be chosen by God because of deeds or heritage. It is simply God's all-powerful choice to save us simply through his mercy, not by our deeds. God's promise to us is that he will save all of us who come to him, through Jesus.

Redemption

You may ask, why is Christ called our redeemer? Remember, sin defined is the disparity between who we are and who we were created to be. The sin that we have lived in for so long has a price tag of death on it. Jesus Christ paid the price on the Cross so that we can go free. Jesus becomes a mediator, so to speak, between God and us. He intercedes on our behalf between God and us. He has redeemed us in God's eyes and we are Holy in his sight. Just as surely as we are redeemed, we are also forgiven and made whole in the eyes of God. This is the idea of Redemption.

Justification

Romans 10:10

"For it is with your heart that you believe and are justified and it is with your mouth that you confess and are saved." (NIV)

So what happens then, you might ask? Well, when we are saved, when we invite Christ into our hearts, we are justified in Christ. Justification is the act of God declaring us "not guilty" for our transgressions or sins. Paul says in Romans 4:25:

"He was delivered over to death for our sins and was raised to life for our justification." (NIV)

The justification process brings peace with God. We have been reconciled to him; there is no longer any sin blocking us from the sunlight of his spirit. In Romans 5:18 Paul goes on to explain:

"Consequently, just as the result of one trespass was the condemnation for all men, so also the result of one act of righteousness was justification that brings life for all men." (NIV)

The one trespass Paul is referring to here is the sin of Adam, the family heritage that leads to certain death. Paul is telling us that even though we all have inherited Adam's sinful nature, God in Christ Jesus has provided us a way out. Now we can trade our sin for God's righteousness. Christ gives us the opportunity to die to our family heritage in Adam and be born again into his spiritual family. This is the function of justification. If you have asked Christ to come into your life, you have it, you are justified, grace is bestowed upon you, and your sins are forgiven. Picture two columns if you will, the first column is your life and transgressions, and the second column is Jesus Christ and his blood on the Cross. God simply takes all your transgressions or sins and places them in Jesus' column and in turn takes the righteousness of Jesus Christ and puts it in your column. Christ paid the penalty for your sin with his blood. Now you have been assigned righteousness. With that righteousness, God gives us the gift of grace and a seed of faith.

In Hebrews 4:16; we read the words:

"Let us then approach the throne of grace with confidence, so that we may receive mercy and find grace to help us in our time of need." (NIV)

To understand the awesome power of this gift, we must first have an understanding of how difficult it was to reach God in Old Testament times. In those times, the high priest could only approach God one time per year. Because of Christ's work on the Cross, we now have direct access to God in prayer through Christ Jesus.

Now our job is to understand that grace, we should live out of that grace, we should not live our lives trying to get it. Grace is the gift, it cannot be earned, and we must learn to train that seed of faith to become a branch of the vine of Christ's righteousness. Here what Jesus says in John 15:1,

"I am the true vine, and my Father is the gardener. He cuts off every branch in me that bears no fruit, while every branch that does bear fruit he prunes so that it can be more fruitful. You are already clean because of the word I have spoken to you. Remain in me, and I will remain in you. No branch can bear fruit by itself; it must remain in the vine. Neither can you bear fruit unless you remain in me. I am the vine; you are the branches. If a man remains in me and I in him, he will bear much fruit; apart from me, you can do nothing."(NIV)

Do you have ears that you can hear these words? Are you beginning to get a picture of who we are? If God is the gardener, Christ is the vine, and we who are in Christ are the branches and we are working in union with the Holy Spirit to be fruitful then we truly are in Christ. We are part of Gods spiritual family. We are now sons and daughters of the living God. Grace has been bestowed and we are part of Gods family now. We are now saints in the eyes of God. We are no longer sinners! Original sin has been removed; remember we were born of Adam, now we are born of the second Adam or Jesus Christ. Paul teaches in Romans5: 18-19,

"Consequently, just as the result of one trespass was condemnation for all men, so also the result of one act of righteousness was justification that brings life for all men. For just as though the disobedience of the one man the many were made sinners, so also through the obedience of the one man the many will be made righteous."(NIV)

In 1 Corinthians 15:21; Paul writes,

"For since death came through a man, the resurrection of the dead comes also through a man. For as in Adam all die, so in Christ all will be made alive."(NIV)

The grace that is bestowed upon us is the gift of forgiveness of sins and the seed of faith that is planted in our hearts. Just as Adam brought sin into the world, so in the same manner Christ overcame sin that we may go free. We are the branches, the body of Christ, we are the church and we are called to reflect Gods glory in all we do.

Sanctification

Now that we are justified in Christ, we immediately begin the lifelong process of sanctification. In Romans 5:1-3; Paul says:

"Therefore since we have been justified in Christ we have peace with God through our Lord Jesus Christ, through whom we have gained access by faith into his grace in which we know stand. And we rejoice in the hope of the glory of God. Not only so, but we rejoice in our sufferings, because we know that suffering produces perseverance, character, and character hope." (NIV)

This is where the Christian life gets difficult at times. Sanctification is the process by which we are called to be pure in heart, to become like Christ through the work of the Holy Spirit. Things tend to get confusing here because in our relationship with Jesus, we have the grace of his presence, but we also have the pressure of the things of this world weighing us down. It is the idea that we are kings in Christ's court but we are slaves to our flesh or our thinking. The flesh or the way we think causes us to sin. To do things we do not want to do. The heritage of Adam burdens our yoke. Sanctification is the process by which we remain steadfast in our commitment to Christ as we walk through countless problems and temptations in this world. It is a continual renewal of the mind or our way of thinking. It is the idea that we must crucify our flesh and our thinking that does not agree with the word of God or the truth. Remember Gods word is truth.

Therefore, we must learn to control our bodily desires and place our heavenly desires above them. We are no longer driven by desire and impulse but, to the contrary, are to live as children of light, not just in public but in private as well. We must live our lives in private just as we do in public.

Now we are in Christ and we are responsible for our actions. Before we act, we must be sure that our foundation is on solid ground. As children of light, our actions must reflect our faith. We must make sure that we understand the consequences of our actions and the importance of what is at stake when we fail to balance our lives between who we say we are in Christ and how we truly live our lives.

Once we enter into the process of sanctification, it is a lifelong process. Many times, it is two steps forward and one step back. The idea is that when we fall into sin we must immediately acknowledge our wrongdoing, ask God for forgiveness, and repent. Paul tells us in 2 Corinthians 7:1:

"Since we have these promises, dear friends, let us purify ourselves from everything that contaminates the body and spirit, perfecting holiness out of reverence for God." (NIV)

Purifying ourselves is a twofold action, which involves turning away from your sin and completely forsaking it.

Action #1 — We must have a change of heart and mind about the matter, we must change the way we think about the sin in our life, we cannot defeat it by trying to pray it away or by abstaining from it we must change the way we think about the thing that is causing us to sin. We, the unrighteous must forsake our thoughts. Remember in order to bear fruit we must strike at the absolute root of the sin. We must remove our personal judgment of others, our distorted thoughts, lustful fantasies, or any other character defect that cause us to sin and seek to sanctify our hearts of these sinful desires. We draw an imaginary line in the sand, so to speak, and say, "From this day forward I will not move past that line, and turn towards God."

Action #2 — To repent of our sins means that we turn away from the sinful way of thinking and we return to the Lord! We turn to God for strength and we command those things that tempt us to flee with the power of the Holy Spirit, which God has placed in our hearts.

Sanctification requires the art of self-examination. Each day we must examine our actions, our relationships, our work, our motives, where we acted inappropriately, if at all and what must be done to correct it. Paul describes this process in 2 Corinthian 13:5. Paul says:

"Examine yourselves to see whether you are in the faith; test yourselves. Do you not realize that Christ Jesus is in you — unless of course, you fail the test?" (NIV)

Here, Paul is urging the Corinthians to check their motives and make sure that they were acting in accordance with their Christian faith. This is a powerful way to grow in the sanctification process because it gives you a way to daily check your spiritual progress and gives you a growing awareness of the power and presence of Christ in your life. Once we have completed this daily inventory, we must be willing to make atonement to whomever we have harmed. We must be willing to go to those persons or entities we have transgressed upon and say we apologize for this. The purpose here is to own our part, to keep our side of the street clean, and be right with God. Their response is not the issue here. What matters to God is your heart and your willingness to set things right, to reflect his glory. This will bring peace to your relationship with God. Let God turn the heart of the person you are concerned with whatever way he will.

Personal Testimony about Making Amends:

I want to share some more personal testimony with you. I think one of the greatest healers in my process of sanctification was my transgression against my last employer before I was saved. At the heart of my disease was the impulsive desire to always get more and that took money. The problem with that is that I never had money because I spent it the minute I got it to support my habits. In the last year of my addiction while working for a company in my hometown, I began to book concerts under the table. When I had the opportunity, I would sell a job and get paid directly. What I was doing was illegal and could have landed me in jail for a long time. When I got sober and the process of the twelve steps began to unfold, I began to get a very uneasy feeling about this. Out of all the petty stealing and deceitful things I had done, none could do me so much harm as this one. In fact, I began to fear that if I did not do something to correct it, I would not be able to stay sober. What I realized was that a fear of not staying sober was the wrong motivation for bringing this out in the open. I needed to do this so I would be right with God. I needed to clean up the wreckage of my past, I needed to go to that person and let him know what I had done and how I intended to correct it.

My will is now aligned with God and this is the proper motivation that guides us through the sanctification process. As God saved me from myself and I began to understand that Jesus died for my sins so that I could go free, I could not help but become emotional. You see, the turning point for me was the pivotal point where I realized that I was not getting clean and setting things right just to stay out of trouble or just to set things right so I would not live in fear. It went much deeper than that. Now I longed for something far greater than anything I had ever experienced before. I wanted to be pure in heart; I wanted to be just like Jesus. I began to hunger to have a heart for Jesus.

I weep when I allow myself to envision Jesus being nailed to the Cross because of my sins. I weep when I envision the pain that he endured so that I could have a relationship with God. This vision ignites my motivation to set the record straight and to live a new life for Jesus. To serve him based on the overwhelming sense of love and gratitude for what he did for me on the Cross, not out of some distorted sense of duty, fear or obligation. Yes, we are in the spirit now and we are motivated by true love.

So upon my return from treatment I had a long list of people I had harmed and was ready to make amends where feasible. The first one on the list was my employer. I had no financial means to pay him back and I was prepared to have him arrest me and send me to jail. I also had to tell my mother what I had done, what I needed to do to be right with God, and I feared that this would be the final straw with her. When I told my mother what I had done, she looked at me with loving eyes and said she would stand behind me. Together we went to my boss and I told him what I had done. He agreed to take a payment from my mother for the number of jobs I had done under the table. My mother paid the debt and I agreed to terms with my mother, in his presence. He was very gracious and understanding and my mother again proved to be God's angel in my life. I did not get into any further trouble and I paid my mother the $1900.00 off in six months, and I had peace over the issue.

The idea of sanctification is the daily practice examining our attitudes and actions and ensuring that we are living by the Spirit. Our new heart demands that we not be at odd with our brother. When we are truly living with a Heart for Jesus we can honestly close our eyes knowing that we have been in Christ that

74

day and we rest peaceably. However, when our examination reveals a problem we must commit to correct in a responsible manner, pray about it, then we rest with a right heart. Jesus tells us in Matthew 5:23-24:

"Therefore if you are offering your gift at the altar and there remember that your brother has something against you, leave your gift there in front of the altar. First go and be reconciled to your brother, then come and offer your gift." (NIV)

Jesus is telling us that we must not be hypocrites. We can not in good faith be right with him and be at odds with our brother. We must make every effort to set the record straight. And then we hear the words of the Apostle John in 1 John 4:20:

"If anyone says "I love God" but hates his brother, he is a liar." (NIV)

John is telling us that if we really want to know where we are in our relationship with God, we should look at where we are in our relationship with those around us. We cannot claim to love God and dislike our Brothers; we cannot claim to love God and gossip about our Brothers and Sisters in Christ. We cannot claim to love God and then try to manipulate others to have our way. We must daily take a hard look in the mirror. We must ensure through the process of self-examination that we are balancing our lives between whom we say we are in Christ and how we actually live.

Glorification

Then the final stage of growth is the Glorification, which is the actual state of the believer after death when we become like Christ.

Through all these terms are many fundamental ideas in scripture about our nature. Once we are saved, we are set free from the laws of sin and death. We have become righteous and Holy in Christ. We are sanctified and made acceptable in Christ. It is the idea that we are not reformed; we are not reeducated or rehabilitated. We are a new creation. Ephesians 1:4 Paul says:

"For he chose us in him before the creation to be holy and blameless in his sight." (NIV)

Because of Christ we are Holy and blameless and covered with God's love. This is what we look like in God's eyes.

How does God measure us against others who may be more spiritually enlightened than we may? How does God view me in relation to another who has been saved longer than I have? Paul says in Galatians 3:28:

"There is neither Jew nor Greek, slave nor free, male nor female, for you are all one in Christ Jesus." (NIV)

It is very important that we all hear this. Paul is telling us that it does not matter who we are or where we are in our faith walk, we must remember that we are one body, and we are all Brothers and Sisters in Christ. We all have gifts and we all are equipped to minister in different ways. It is now our duty as new Christians to find out what our gifts are and how we can use them. It is the duty of the more mature Christians in the Church to minister to those still searching and equip them for service.

Now that we have a fundamental understanding of our nature in Christ, it is equally important that we look at how we walk through this process of transformation, how we persevere through the troubles and trials of the Christian life. Yes, we must explore the idea of good decision-making and what the foundations of sound Godly decisions are based on.

Chapter 5 Study Guide

Q1: Share some good and bad decisions you have made and how they have affected others!

Q2: How do we make God centered decisions?

Q3: Please explain in your own words how God views us!

Q4: Explain how you feel about having direct access to God once you are saved!

Q5: Are you taking time to be with God? Please elaborate!

Q6: Explain the idea of repentance!

Q7: As honestly as you can describe the person that you are becoming when you see yourself in the mirror!

Chapter 6

A Ride to the Airport

Sin will take you farther than you want to go!
Sin will keep you longer than you want to stay!
Sin will cost you more than you want to pay!
                                    —Anonymous

Brother Carl, I am sitting in the St. Louis airport reflecting on the gift God gave me this morning. He introduced me to you. Yes for twenty-two minutes from the hotel to the airport, God departed wisdom on me beyond my years. Let me share this story with you.

Not too long ago I was leaving a business conference, The Green Industry exposition, for which I am a proud participant. I awoke to a vigorous prayer time on my knees with God that morning. The Holy Spirit was moving through me and I was feeling all the passion of days of learning and growing in business and in my personal time with God. You see I spent every waking moment, I was not in seminars, chasing scripture and writing this book. I cried out to God in gratitude for the gifts of the past few days. I told God how badly I missed my wife and children and asked him to please bless the flights I would be on that would take me home that day.

I had called ahead to get a cab and the lady at the front desk phoned to say the Cab Co., car #7, would be picking me up in fifteen minutes. When I walked out the front door, it was as if I had entered an open market. Cab drivers were fighting for my business and I went directly to the Cab Co. car #7.

As, I got into Carl's cab, Carl was shaking his head and another cab driver was still trying to coax me into his vehicle. As we drove away, I looked at Carl and said, "Wow, is it always this tough for you out here?" He said, "Yes, but de way I see it is this, every day God sends me out fishin', but he never promised me I would catch something." What wisdom, I thought, and off we went into a conversation about God. I mentioned faith and that sometimes God just wants us to trust that things will be OK. With that comment, he shared something even more valuable to me. He said, "My wife is the biggest part of my faith; she always believes and pulls me through, but the thing is it took me so long to understand her. In fact it took me a lot of pain and two marriages to understand a woman."

He went on to share that one time about thirty years ago, he told his daddy that he did not understand women and that he may have to leave his wife and his dad said, "Son, sit down, need you mind 'bout understandin' no women, it ain't yor job to understand a woman. It's yor job to love her." Please excuse my spelling, but I am trying to be accurate about the portrayal of events. He went on to explain that his dad told him, "Naw, ain't no need to understand a woman. Why do you think God put Adam to sleep when he made Eve? Naw, we ain't supposed to understand no women. God jest wants us to love 'em."

By now, I had a smile a mile wide and I was soaking up the conversation. It was a gift from God and I knew it, as did he. At this point, I had to stop him and ask if I could write down his words. He agreed, so I did. We went on to the airport and he revealed several other pieces of wisdom I would have never learned from a book. He shared his salvation, his faith, and God's grace in his life with me, and most importantly the process of growth in his life. Then he went on to ask me, "You know what they say about change, don't you?" And as I said, "I sure do" we both recited the slogan together,

"Change is inevitable. Growth is optional."
— Anonymous

As our trip to the airport was complete, we smiled upon one another, shook hands, and praised God for the time we had shared. As I walked away, I felt that I had briefly encountered the true spirit of Christ that morning in a man who did not have much in the way of money, but had everything in the way of the kind of prosperity that only God through Christ Jesus can provide. He had peace, joy, and contentment, plenty of family to love at home, and a long list of Brothers and Sisters in Christ at his church.

You see, when we are first saved, when we are justified, when we become righteous in God's eyes, we are a new creation. All we have known is dead to us. For the first time we see the world God has created through new eyes? Can you imagine seeing life from a completely new perspective? Well, you do not have to imagine it. If you have asked Jesus to come into your heart, which I pray you have by now, then you are that new creature. You have been transformed. The old has gone the new has begun. You now have a Heart for Jesus. Now it is time to go out into the world and do what we are called to do as Christians.

What are we called to do? We are to let Jesus live out his life through us! We are to be a witness of God's transforming grace and spread the good news of the Gospel. We are to serve and minister to others. Most importantly, the time has come for us to test our new wings. It is time to truly seek the living water and the bread of life. In order to grow we must train and strengthen our hearts, a baby must train his legs to become stronger as he trains himself to walk and we are just like that child when we are born again through faith in Jesus Christ. How do your muscles get stronger? You train them! How do run farther? You train, do you not? How do we develop a heart for Jesus? That is correct! We train our minds to agree with the truth or the word of God. We cannot delay we absolutely without a doubt must go into training for the renewing of our minds and our attitudes.

Carl thanks you for your heart, your witness of Gods grace in your life, and your testimony of transformation. I wish I could express the immense amount of gratitude that overwhelmed my heart that day. I could not wait to sit down and find a place for this short story in this book. Carl displayed the essence of evangelism. He put himself out there, he moved out of his comfort zone, he spoke about God and witness of his sovereign majesty and grace to someone he did not know. Jesus calls us to spread the Good News of the Gospel. Carl did this so well and with an amazing sense of humility. Thank you Lord for this brief encounter and thanks again Carl for wisdom beyond my years.

Chapter 6 Study Guide

Q1: What is your attitude towards your work?

Q2: How much importance do you place on work?

Q3: Do you understand your spouse?

Q4: Are you more concerned with loving your spouse the way God loves you or getting what you think you need?

Q5: How can you change your attitudes and actions towards your spouse to create a more God centered marriage?

Q6: Please share a great God Story! I would love to hear them. Email me at thall37@carolina.rr.com.

Chapter 7

Going Into Training

"Do you know that in a race all the runners run, but only one gets the prize? Run in such a way as to get the prize. Everyone who competes in the games goes into strict training. They do it to get a crown that will not last, but we do it to get a crown that will last forever. Therefore I do not run like a man running aimlessly, I do not fight like a man beating the air. No, I beat my body, and make it my slave so that after I have preached to others I will not be disqualified for the prize." (NIV)

1 Corinthians 9:24-27

To run the race of the Christian life takes hard work, because we are training our bodies to live in sync with our new nature. Remember the heart for Jesus that we have acquired. Not forgetting that the reason we train our bodies is to defeat the old nature that regularly surfaces, the sinful nature, born of Adam. We must continually beat our bodies into submission and not act on its impulsive desires. How many of us act daily on what our bodies tell us to do. I know I do. I am aware of it and trying to train my body to do what Gods word would have me do. You see, in our sinful nature or old life when our body wanted something we acted on it. When I lusted I acted, when I craved I ate, when I desired to drink alcoholically I drank, when I saw something I wanted, I bought it. These are the old ways, actions without regards to consequences. Paul is giving us a glimpse of what we are training for. We, unlike the runners in a race, all get the prize of a crown that will last forever. Therefore, we should be purposeful and deliberate about our training and our transformation. Paul has given us the goal; now it is up to us to develop the discipline.

Before we spread our wings and fly, let us talk about a few things. I have flown many times only to fall and lose my wings, or should I say my desire to fly as a new Christian, because I did not have my true north identified. My failure was that I just jumped off the cliff and began to fly without charting a course. I just wanted to be the best person I could be. I wanted to be a productive member of society. I wanted to fly and serve God.

So, what was missing in my life that caused my wings to sputter? What took the wind out of my sails? It was a lack of direction and a lack of knowledge regarding the process of sanctification. It was a lack of sound Godly wisdom and spiritual discipline to become more like Christ. As I began to fly, I felt as though I was on a reward and good work type of flight and that as long as I did good God would love me. I felt like I had to keep every moral law I had ever read plus another 2,000 I heard about and what is worse I kept placing more restrictions on myself to prevent further failings. From the beginning of my flight, I lacked understanding about who I was. I was living by a rewards for good behavior philosophy of my relationship with Christ and I was living out a code of morals that kept me proud when I did good and filled with shame when my flesh took over my will to be Christ like and I would sin.

Eventually I began to ask myself the big question. If I am really saved, if I am really a Christian, why do I keep sinning? Why do I still have a desire to sin? Even though I have been saved, I still have a desire to sin. As we discussed earlier our old nature will not just go away. Our hearts are transformed and we have a heart for Jesus now, but our bodies need to be disciplined. It is the idea that we will no longer let our bodies tell us what to do, but to the contrary, we will tell our bodies what they will do.

OK, so how do we do it, you may ask. How do we discipline our bodies? What does it look like?

Through the process of sanctification we have learned the principle of Ephesians 4:22-24, where we take off the clothing from our old nature, we renew our minds by changing our focus and our attitudes, and we dress ourselves in the clothing of our new nature. That is the discipline of our training and then Paul gives us a picture of what our discipline will entail in Ephesians 4:25-5:21:

"Therefore each one of you must put off falsehood and speak truthfully to his neighbor, for we are all members of one body. In your anger do not sin: Do not let the sun go down while you are still angry and do not give the devil a foothold. He who has been stealing must steal no longer, but must work doing something useful with his own hands, that he may have something to share with those in need. Do not let any unwholesome talk come out of your mouths, but only what is helpful for building others up according to their needs, that it may benefit those who listen. And do not grieve the Holy Spirit of God, with whom you were sealed for the day of redemption. Get rid of all bitterness, rage and anger, brawling and slander, along with every form of malice. Be kind and compassionate to one another, forgiving each other, just as in Christ God forgave you. Be imitators of God, therefore as dearly loved children and live a life of love just as Christ loved us and gave himself up for us as a fragrant offering and sacrifice to God. But among you there must not be even a hint of sexual immorality, or of any kind of impurity, or of greed, because these are improper for God's holy people. Nor should there be any obscenity, foolish talk or course joking, which are out of place, but rather thanksgiving. For this you can be sure no immoral, impure or greedy person—such a man is an idolater — has any inheritance in the kingdom of Christ and God. Let no one deceive you with empty words, for because of such things God's wrath comes on those who are disobedient. Therefore do not be partners with them. For you were once in darkness, but now you are light in the Lord. Live as Children of light, for the fruit of the light consists in all goodness, righteousness, and truth and find out what pleases the Lord. Have nothing to do with the fruitless deeds of darkness, but rather expose them. For it is shameful to even mention what the disobedient do in secret. But exposed by the light becomes visible, for it is light that makes everything visible, That is why it is said, Wake up O sleeper, rise from the dead, and Christ will shine on you. Be very careful then, how you live — not as unwise but as wise, making the most of every opportunity, because the days are evil. Therefore do not be foolish but understand what the Lord's will is. Do not get drunk on wine, which leads to debauchery. Instead be filled with the spirit. Speak to one another with psalms, hymns, and spiritual songs. Sing and make music in your heart to the Lord, always giving thanks to God the Father for everything, in the name of our Lord Jesus Christ. Submit to one another out of reverence for Christ. (NIV)

If you skipped it, please go back and chew on it. Make a list for yourself. Paul has given us an accurate snapshot of what we must endure and train for in the transformation process. If we are to truly live as children of light, as we are called to here, we must train our bodies so that our beliefs matches our behavior. We must balance our lives between what God has put in us and how we live out our each day. In 1 Timothy 4:7-8, Paul tells us:

"Having nothing to do with godless myths and old wives tales, rather train yourself to be godly. For physical training is of some value, but godliness has value for all things, holding promise for both the present life and the life to come." (NIV)

If you had a choice between doing physical exercise and spiritual exercise, which would you choose? I am certainly not advocating the lack of physical training. The Lord knows how I could stand to lose a few pounds. However, in the end what becomes more valuable to you? Is the development of your physical being going to sustain you better, in times of trouble, than the training of your faith? Isn't it imperative that we find time now to begin training and developing our spiritual muscle?

Developing Spiritual Muscle!

We do this by creating spiritual discipline in our lives, through the working out of our spiritual muscles. In order to work our spiritual muscle it is imperative that we stretch our minds by getting into the word of God! That is right! We read the Bible, we read books about God, we study his sovereignty, we study his grace, and then we apply it to our lives.

If we want to see transformation take place in our lives, if we want to change, then we must begin by disciplining our hearts. Let us start out by defining Godly discipline.

Godly discipline should be defined as the ability to create a personal vision for our lives that is God centered and is in accordance with God's will. Then by faith, we act on the empowerment of the Holy Spirit and we turn from the self-serving, self-destructive lifestyle behaviors that lead to sin and, turn to those behaviors that lead to eternal life. Read what Paul has to say about grace in Titus 2:11-12:

"For the grace of God that brings salvation has appeared to all men. It teaches us to say "No" to ungodliness and worldly passions, and to live self-controlled, upright and godly lives in this present age," (NIV)

In my life, I continually try to develop spiritual muscle by following the process below. These five areas of our lives need to be written down, discussed, prayed over, discussed in a small group setting or with a spiritual partner, and then we should measure our progress.

The five areas of Godly Discipline are:

1) Developing a spirit of love in our hearts
2) Identifying Godly Goals for our lives
3) Developing Godly self-control
4) Developing a Spirit of Godly motivation
5) Developing a Spirit of Godly persistence

Let's look at these in some detail.

Developing a Spirit of Love in Our Hearts:

John 3:16; says;
"For God so loved the world that he gave his one and only Son, that whoever believes in him shall not perish but have eternal life." (NIV)

This is where it all begins! This is perfect love! This is sacrificial love. I believe that many of us think we love others, but do we truly love, as we should? Many of us, without realizing it, fall far short of the mark here, myself included. Do we love only those who love us? Do we say we love our Brother or Sister and then talk about them when they walk away? Do we say we love God, but fail to seek him? Do we love money and material things more than God? Do we use the word "love" all too freely, without truly understanding the implications of what we are saying? Do we love our neighbors as ourselves? That is a hard one!

Love, defined, is a strong affection for a person, spirit, or thing; it is a desire or devotion so strong that it overcomes all things. I do not intend to ignite a discussion about the different types and degrees of love here. My purpose is to get us to look at our hearts. We must understand that the true indication of the love in our hearts will be how we think, feel and act every day towards others. This type of unconditional love must be at the root of our hearts. It is the kind of love that puts others first, it means being unselfish. Loving others means giving sacrificially of our time and money to others who are in need.

Love is the central theme of 1 John. We get a picture of love as the guiding force in our lives. It is the guiding force that offers health, healing, wholeness, and a sense of direction in our lives. We learn in 1 John how to measure where we are in our relationship with God by looking at how we treat others. If you want to know whether or not you are maturing spiritually then you can measure your growth by how you respond to others in Christ. Are you being understanding or judgmental? Are you sowing discord or harmony in relationships? Are you giving or just taking? These are the hard questions we must ask of ourselves if we are to grow in Christ. There is not one of us who does not take two steps forward and one step back in this area. We trust, we get hurt, we build walls! Then we tear down and we gossip. It is critical that we focus on the solutions in life and not the problems. When we fall, we must:

1. introspectively evaluate our shortcomings,
2. clean up our mistakes in love and without expectation
3. continue in our journey to develop a heart for Jesus.

Remember, in Ephesians Paul teaches us that we must be patient, humble, and gentle, and we must bear up with one another in love. This is the sacrificial other centered love that Paul was talking about. Paul is trying to tell us that it is not about US, but in fact when we take our minds off ourselves and focus on how we can help others, we reflect Gods glory. Then, people will see God in us and they will want to know this God that guides are hearts.

Therefore, at the root of our hearts we must cultivate a true love of others. I am not talking about a physical love or a love of what they look like, how they dress, speak, or the house or car they have. No, I am talking a spiritual love that accepts unconditionally. The kind of love that Paul speaks of in 1 Corinthians 13:4:

"Love is patient, love is kind. Love does not envy, it does not boast, it is not proud. It is not rude, it is not self seeking, it is not easily angered, it keeps no record of wrongs. Love does not delight in evil but rejoices in truth. It always protects, always trusts, always hopes, always perseveres." (NIV)

Paul is giving us a picture of how we can develop the kind of perfect love that God offers us. We learned earlier that love is the action that we take in serving others. It is the by-product of the grace we have received in Christ Jesus. It becomes the motivator by which we ensure that God's word will not return to him empty!

So would it be fair to say that 1 John 4:17 shall be the foundation of our hearts:

"God is love. Whoever lives in love lives in God, and God in him." (NIV)

This is the heart of the matter, the core of having a heart for Jesus. If we operate our lives out of worry, fear, discord, anger, resentment, malice, vengeance, or any other type of self-serving motivator, then we are not on the right path. We do not understand who we are in Christ and who God is unless we operate out of a spirit of love and service towards others. Don't

89

you see that we are learning to agree with Gods word, which is truth, we are learning to live by the Holy Spirit. How many scripture talk of love and how we can grow in love? 1 John 4:18, says:

"There is no fear in love. But, perfect love drives out fear because fear has to do with punishment. The one who fears is not made perfect in love."(NIV)

We grow in love by trusting the outcomes of our loving actions to God. We grow in love by letting go of the fear that keeps us in our comfort zones. In other words, even though we know someone may respond negatively towards are phone call to welcome them or to talk or they may just plain ignore our phone call and make up an excuse as to why they did not call you back, it really does not matter. Don't you see? You reached out to someone in love because that is what God would have you do. You see, it is not the response you receive that is important. It is the action you take that brings God joy! I do not know about you, but the words, " well done, good and faithful servant" drive me. After everything the Lord has blessed me with, the least I can do is reach out to others. When asked and meditated upon, God will quiet our fears and give us the confident assurance we need to love his way!

Remember, the essence of our lives as Christians is building up the body of Christ. We are to keep the unity of the spirit through the bond of peace. We are to practice humble, other-centered relationships. We are to love one another! 1 John 4:17, says:

"Dear friends, let us love one another, for love comes from God. Everyone who loves has been born of God and knows God. Whoever does not love does not know God, because God is love. (NIV)

Let us pray together that we may grow in the spirit of love!

PRAYER

Father God, we lift our hearts to you in humble gratitude for the grace you have bestowed upon us. We ask that you would spread your love about our hearts and help us to cultivate the seeds of love, which you have so graciously placed in the fertile soil of our new hearts. Father, grant that the Holy Spirit will guide us as we learn to be motivated by true love for you and not out of duty, fear or obligation. Father we praise your sovereign grace and glory. Amen!

With the new wineskin of love surrounding our hearts we must commence the journey down the road of developing the remaining Godly principles needed to continue our transformation. We must put new wine into our wineskins now. If we try to put our sinful nature into our new heart, the wine skin will burst! Jesus tells us in Matthew 9:17:

"Neither do men pour new wine into old wineskins. If they do, the skins will burst, the wine will run out and the wineskins will be ruined. No, they pour new wine into new wineskins and both are preserved." (NIV)

The idea is that in order for us to experience the fruit of the spirit, we must develop roots first.

Identifying Godly Goals in Our Lives

Paul tells us in Galatians 5:16:

"So I say, live by the spirit, and you will not gratify the desires of the sinful nature." (NIV)

91

and then in Galatians 5:22; Paul tells us,

"But the fruit of the Spirit is love, joy, peace, patience, kindness, goodness, faithfulness, gentleness and self-control."(NIV)

So, how do we identify Godly goals? How do we live by the spirit? First, we identify the primary goal. Paul has given us the primary goal in Galatians 5:22.

The Primary Goal : We want to reap the fruit of the spirit.

Now that we have the result we desire, we must identify the process by which we achieve these goals.

The Process: we must live by the Spirit

Paul tells us in Galatians 5:16 that we must live by the spirit so that we do not gratify our old sinful nature.

OK, how do I live by the spirit? I had the same question. Now that we know who we are in Christ, we understand the process by which we are saved, and we are ready to serve God out of LOVE, not obligation or duty, we look at our Godly Goals. First, we must ask ourselves:

How do I become a child of God? What does my life look like when it is aligned with the will of God? How do I live by the Spirit? We must prioritize our lives. We must arrange our lives in such a way that we would honor Gods word, which is truth. We live by the spirit through developing a personal relationship with God, taking care of our family and training them in the ways of God, earning a living to support our families and our church. Serving in ministry areas in our church home and finally allowing personal time to refresh our spirit through personal hobbies, quiet time with God, exercise, or sports. We must do this in a balanced way that leads to a productive and balanced lifestyle that reflects who we are in Christ.

After quite a bit of reflection and adjustment through the years, my God centered and balanced life looks like this.

As a business owner, a father of two children, a husband, personal needs, ministry needs, writing, playing golf, working, employees, etc. My cry to God for so long has been, "How, God, how do I balance life's yoke?" What I have learned to do is to say, "OK, God. Here we are and here is my calendar. Please help me define my spiritual goals. Help me to identify what it means to be a child of God in your eyes." Off I go with my calendar, which is actually my outlook on my computer. It is great because it memorizes recurring appointments. What I do is determine what my life would look like if I were truly the man God wanted me to be. How would I prioritize my life?

This is what it looks like in order of priority:

1) God
2) Spouse
3) Family
4) Work
5) Ministry
6) Personal time
7) God

See, that wasn't so hard, was it? What I have done is I have decided that in my life this is going to be the good orderly direction (GOD) that will reflect God's will for my life. How do I know this is God's will for my life? If you take a bit of time to study the letter to the church of Colosse and the letter to the Church at Ephesus, you will find some implicit instruction from God on how we should balance the different areas of our lives. In Chapter 3 & 4 of Colossians, Paul devotes several paragraphs to rules for Holy living. He describes for us what Christians should do to live a Godly life and then he proceeds to describe rules for Christian homes. Now granted, it does not say to follow them in this order, but they are primary examples of how we should relate to each other.

Remember, if we want to be successful in other-centered relationships, we must begin in our tent. Our tent is the body in which we live. Our homes and our tent can keep our hearts hidden from others. However, there is not a place we can hide our hearts from God. I believe Paul has placed the order of things here because he had divine wisdom. I have tried to order my life differently and it only produces chaos. It produces a life that is lived under pressure. When our lives are disciplined as Paul discusses, we begin to live our lives under priority.

As if this was not enough to make you a believer, we then look at the letter to the Church at Ephesus. In Chapter 5, Paul again begins with the similar instruction on how to live for Christ. He then places a great deal of importance on the relationship between the husband and wife. He then goes on to describe in detail the relationships between children and parents, finally slaves and masters.

I do not know about you, but the order of things becomes quite apparent. Paul is giving us the idea that one builds upon another. It is the idea that we must take God into our day, all day, every day. No matter where you are or what you do, there shall never be a reason why you cannot start your day with God. When you get up, kiss your wife, grab your coffee, go to a quiet place and be with God. Walk into your day with the peace of God and his grace will abound in your life. Leave God on the shelf and you will quickly be overcome with worldly clamor.

In Mark 1:35 we read:

"Very early in the morning, while it was still dark, Jesus got up, left the house and went off to a solitary place, where he prayed." (NIV)

If Christ made time for his Father in Heaven, if the Lamb of God, the only person to ever walk the Earth without sin, made prayer and quiet time early in the morning a Godly priority in his life, then how much more do we need it in our lives? So let us explore my Godly prioritized life.

#1 God

For me, the first and foremost thing I need in my life is a strong relationship with God. So a long time ago I decided that God was going to be the first person I talked to every day. I decided that when I get up each day I am going to get on my knees and pray, then I am going to spend the next twenty minutes to a maximum of one hour reading the Bible, studying scripture, and meditating on his word.

Let me give you an accurate picture of meditation here. I think the term meditation has been completely obliterated and misused in our culture. I have heard all kinds of descriptions of how people meditate, from clearing your mind out and thinking of nothing; boy, that one is really hard and pointless. I have heard that we should burn incense and say, "OHMMMM." I have also heard it said that prayer is talking to God and meditating is listening for his answer. I could go on and on, but I will spare you. So let's get back to Godly meditation.

The Biblical definition for meditation is:
"to contemplate, to think deeply about."(NIV)

I spend time five days a week meditating on the word. Saturdays I allow myself to rest and Sunday we go to church. Often times I will watch Charles Stanley, take notes and then go to church. I conclude my morning time with God, with a prayer that he may show me, throughout the day, how to best apply his word to my walk and help me to balance my life between who I say I am in Christ and how I live.

For me the first one is not difficult because I know the grace and blessings that abound when I walk into my day on the shoulders of the Lord. I also know what happens to me if I do not start my day with God. I race into the day, I try to fix everything and everybody, I try to get everybody to do what I want, I end up getting frustrated, I get a bad phone call or a contract cancellation, and I go from financially somewhat fit to bankrupt in a blink of an eye. Do you hear what I am saying? Yes, when I do not start my day with God it does not go very well. I usually operate out of fear and I have no sense of balance; everything becomes a fire drill. When I start my day out with God, he walks with me in everything I do, and even though I run into the things of this world; all the problems, frustration, anger, lust etc., I am much more capable of reconciling my flesh or my thinking, to my faith when I walk out the door with God fresh on my heart.

Therefore, I go to my calendar and I fill up all those spaces from 5 a.m. to 5:40 a.m. Monday through Friday. That is God's time and boy do I protect it. I will tell you this much, it is the best habit I have never needed to quit. Knowledge of the Holy one and the desire to know God better has ignited a passion in my life that I never dreamed possible. Candidly speaking, it is the reason I am writing this book.

#2 Wife
You can probably guess that #2 was a must. I want to personally speak to my wife and let her know how sorry I am for all the times that I have been completely insensitive to her needs when she has called me at work. I am the world's worst at not being able to shift gears when something of a personal nature occurs at work. It is as if I am racing against an invisible ghost to

96

get everything I possibly can get done in the shortest possible amount of time and when I get interrupted I get frustrated or I do not want to be bothered. My spouse is my spiritual partner; she is the one who suffers the most because she is usually the last one to get any of my time and the first one to deal with my daily frustrations. I am struggling in this area, and am daily committed to the call to give her the priority in my life that she deserves. Since my spouse is already in the family time slot, we had to carve out special time for us to be alone together. We plan to have date night every second weekend. This is time for us to play together. We also have our couple's small group time, which is great. Then there is always the not-so-often times that we are able to sneak a few minutes of peace and quiet when the kids are not around, ha ha. So there is #2.

#3 Children

OK, so how do you determine what is # 3? Well, for me this one was not as easy. I went back and forth with work, spouse, and children, trying to justify which was more important. Already understanding the Scripture and how it ordered these areas, I was still struggling, so I began to quietly listen to my heart. Well, that triggered a swell of emotion for me. For many years, I have placed work ahead of my family and I would always feel the pain of not being there. Have you ever missed your child's game because you were to busy, have you ever placed a potential nonpaying client in front of your children's needs? Every single week I am tested on this. You see, every week I get much-appreciated calls from well-meaning potential clients who want me to come to their houses on Saturday when they are off work to look at the jobs that they want done. After many years of doing this, it became apparent to me that my priorities were way out of balance. What were the consequences of my working every Saturday morning? Well, I was giving up the one free day every week to spend with my family, and the message I was sending my wife and my children was they were not as important as my work. I had a serious decision to make. I was facing the fear of not having enough work to cover all the financial obligations I had signed on for, or making a God centered decision to spend much-needed time with my family and trust that God would provide. I prayed over it and made a decision to change. Now when I am asked, sometimes I cringe, but I remain faithful to the decision and I do not back down. I tell potential clients I am available Monday through Friday from seven to five, and that Saturdays are reserved for my family and Sunday is for God and family. I did make the change and God continues to bless.

In fact, that one small change has had a tremendous effect on the financial stability of the business as well as in the minds of our team members. We all know that the weekend is family time and we all work our hardest to ensure that each one of has that time off. It creates a nice company culture. That is another story.

So as all these thoughts were running through my mind, I recalled some scripture from 1 Timothy 3:4:

"He must manage his family well and see that his children obey him with proper respect." (NIV)

What I heard Paul telling me here is that if I desire to have my family be led by the Spirit then I most focus on leading my family with spiritual muscle and I cannot do that when I allow work to take precedence over them, not to mention how Ephesians and Colossians order our priorities for us! Therefore, my family occupies my 5:30 to 8 p.m. time slot Monday through Friday, as well as the Saturday and Sunday time slot. I leave home before they wake up in the morning, so I do not see them then. Therefore, that is how I arrived at my personal God centered priority #3.

98

#4 Work

You probably guessed # 4. Work, that is right, I said it again, that four-letter word. Well, I happen to be blessed with a career that is inspired by God.

Personal Testimony about My Work

When I got clean and sober, the people at the treatment facility told me that one in ten people who had been in my group would stay sober for longer than a year. They also told me that if I went back to the type of work that I was in that my chances of staying sober would be even less. "Wow," I said, "thanks for the encouragement." The reality was that change is always rooted in the truth. The truth was, I could not lead a godly life in the work I was doing. I was not mature enough in my faith. Therefore, I left that line of work and went back into the landscape business. I had spent many years in high school and college working in the maintenance departments and had developed a sort of passion for the outdoors and landscape work. Another wonderful gift in my life is that after approximately a year of working for other people, God presented me with the opportunity to start my own business. In all the time that I was landscaping I found true peace with God, kneeling there in the soil planting flowers and grading the land.

Naturally, getting a business off the ground and balancing life's demands is not an easy task. With a child on the way and a mortgage and bills to pay, my work continued to escalate. Nonetheless, it was critical that I balance this demand in my life from a Godly perspective.

Well, we understand now that change is rooted in truth, and for me the truth of the matter is what value do I place on earning money. Do I put it ahead of my family and ahead of God? I am ashamed to admit that for many years as a young

Christian I placed far more value on getting ahead financially than I did on knowing God. As a result, some scriptural promises occurred during my faith walk. In Psalm 11:28,

Solomon writes:

"Whoever trusts in his riches will fall but the righteous will thrive like a green leaf." (NIV)

In about the beginning of my fourth year of business we were doing extremely well, God had blessed our work, and we had an abundance of work. Yet, I began to trust in riches more than I trusted in God. I began to be motivated by the idea that bigger was better and I wanted more. Yes, I wanted more and for the wrong reasons. Therefore, I began doing work that I was not experienced at quoting and buying more equipment and vehicles than I could stand to pay for. To top it all off, I hired employees at will, with no systems in place to handle the new business, the new employees and the new growth. To anyone with business knowledge, I am sure they would agree that, what I was doing was a recipe for disaster. Well, we grew all right, from half a million in sales to 1.2 million in sales in one year. We went from nine employees to twenty-six employees. The result was pure and simple chaos. I had failed to properly plan for this kind of growth because I was ignorant of the process.

I have come to know three realms of information in my journey.

1) What I know
2) What I know I do not know
3) What I do not know that I do not know

The final one is the most dangerous one of all. I am not going to get any further off track here, but I want to circle back around to

100

the finer point of this matter. We all know we cannot serve two masters. Jesus speaks of this in Matthew. We also know that the desire for money is normal, but when it is pursued in excess or compulsively it becomes idolatry. When we place money above our desire to grow in our relationship with Christ, we are saying that I trust in money more than I trust in God to provide what he feels I am worthy of being blessed with. The point of this story is that in my personal walk to be like Christ my feet traveled down the wrong path. I began to put my trust and my heart's desire in money and I began to operate in the realm of what I did not know that I did not know.

Well, God definitely got my attention here. The Sovereign Gardener was getting ready to do some serious pruning on me! Midway into the fifth year of my business, I got very sick. For about two weeks before I went into the hospital, I was having these crazy pains in my stomach. They finally brought me to my knees; I ended up in the hospital and was critical for several days. What happened, to this day, no one really understands. The doctors could not explain it. I underwent dozens of tests and remained in serious condition for 5 days and then began getting better. To this day only God knows what happened.

God had a different plan. I was working sixteen hours a day before I got sick and everything that God had given me in my new walk with Christ had become devalued. I had come to place more importance on financial prosperity than on my relationship with Christ. I was in the hospital for eight days and they never did determine what was wrong with me, but they almost lost me.

It was another wakeup call for me and I do not think that I have too many left. What I did in my addictions to alcohol I also ended up doing in my walk with Christ. I became addicted to work and success in business, with a continual lusting for more.

The person that walked out of that hospital was a new man, prepared again to do battle with his shortcomings and dedicated to living a life that was driven by Godly principles.

So let us bring this thing full circle. In our relationship with Christ, how can we know if we are getting of course unless we have set up a chart of Godly disciplines and then measure our successes and failures? How can we truly balance our lives between who we say we are in Christ and how we live our lives unless we honestly identify our goals and train ourselves to be disciplined in our walk? If we assume that we know best are we not operating in that area called, "I don't know what I don't know," and are we not redefining God? If we are not setting up a discipline in our lives that allows us to meditate upon his word and gain knowledge of God, then are we really saying, "I will take my chances with God; I really do not care what I do not know." And if we really do not care what we do not know, nor show any motivation to gain knowledge of our God, then are we truly in the sanctification process or have we temporarily checked out to follow some personal desires that do not line up with God's will for our lives? And if this is the case for you then are you not living by the flesh or your own thinking, and are you not trusting in your own strength instead of relying on God

Proverbs gives us literally dozens of scriptures about protecting our hearts and gaining wisdom and knowledge of God. I wish I had possessed the wisdom of this Scripture before I plunged my business into chaos and turmoil. Proverbs 23:4:

"Do not wear yourself out to get rich, have the wisdom to show restraint. Cast but a glance at riches and they are gone, for they will surely sprout wings and fly off to the sky like an eagle."(NIV)

Proverbs 3:13-18

102

"Blessed is the man who finds wisdom, the man who gains understanding, for she is more profitable than silver and yields better returns than gold, She is more Precious than rubies, nothing you desire can compare with her, Long life is in her right hand, in her left hand are riches and honor. Her ways are pleasant ways and all her paths are peace. She is the tree of life to those who embrace her, those who lay hold of her will be blessed." (NIV)

Remember, the tree of life that Adam and Eve ate from was forbidden. Here Solomon is giving us a hint as to how we can begin to think God's thoughts and begin to straighten our paths and make our ways line up with God's ways. You see in order to develop a heart for Jesus we must decide that no matter what happens in life we are going to agree with Gods word, the truth.

Well business is fine now. God and I have got things worked out. Oh, yes there are always good days and bad days but the peace of God surrounds me and I trust in the Lord and I believe he will bless me as he sees fit. Often times I still get caught up in fear, but now I am quickly resolved to my faith. I have allotted 6 a.m. to 5 p.m. Monday through Friday in my calendar for work. I know it seems a bit much. Read on! So that sums up #4.

#5 Ministry
OK, I know what you are saying. "Your schedule is full." Well, let's first define Ministry.

"It is the exercising of one's spiritual gifts and resources to serve and assist others in the building up of the body of Christ."

Your ministry can be performed in many ways, which we will not get into at this time. However, it is imperative that you

103

find out your spiritual gifts and that you use them in your ministry to serve Christ. As you may have noted I have fifty-five hours a week carved out for work. Of that time, I have allotted four hours per week for ministry time. Then I allow time on Sunday as well. Some important things to remember about ministry are:

- Be sure that you keep your priorities balanced when agreeing to serve God in an additional capacity.
- Whatever time you have allotted in your schedule for ministry is the time you can put towards that ministry. If you feel the call so strongly to work in another ministry area, it would be mandatory that you look at your schedule and determine what you are going to take time away from to do it.
- Be sure to align your ministry with your spiritual gifts.
- Remember why you are there — to serve Christ and for the equipping of the saints, in order that we may build up the body of Christ.
- Be sure to keep your cool in all situations; do not react, but pause when you are knocked off balance by circumstance; ask for some time to evaluate, discern, and pray over tensions that arise.
- When crisis occurs, walk in faith and always act with compassion.
- Always be vigilant in expediting your duties.
- Most importantly — serve God in all you do with a grateful heart.

I hesitate to share this with you but I will. These aforementioned suggestions come from a Scripture basis but also from firsthand experience. I want you to know how much I love God and that when he calls I have stood at attention. Again, in my life I seem to keep crossing the rivers of failure.

Some Personal Testimony about My Ministry Work:

Some five years ago after I got sick and refocused my walk with Christ, I began to feel a strong call to serve God. My wife and I began searching and could not seem to find a place to fit in. Well, after a lot of searching, we were driving down the road one afternoon and we saw a sign for a new start-up church. We both looked at each other and said, "Maybe this is where God needs us to serve." Well, we went to the service the following week and every week thereafter for about two months. Then we decided to transfer our membership and continued on our journey at our new church. It was an exciting time for our children and us.

We did what you have to do when you go to a new church. You cannot just sit around and wait to be a part of the church. You have to stick your hand out there and meet people. You have to sign up to help in areas of ministry. Well, needless to say we were off and running. We had developed many great relationships, both my wife and I had given Testimony, we were both involved in small groups and then the unthinkable happened.

Yes, I was completely shaken. I was serving in far too many capacities and spending some twenty hours a week doing service work between all the different ministries I was involved in. I was having bad back problems and doing a lot of heavy lifting for the set up and tear down of the services and had become heavily involved with the Staff Parish Relations Committee on top of ushering and helping run the men's group, and writing devotions. Well you can already tell that I did not follow Godly principles here.

Then, as all churches do, we ran into some growth problems. Some things took place that did not align with what my vision of God's church was and I walked away. Yes, I quit. Somehow, what I was discerning in my time with God is, make a stand and force the change. Well, let's just say I did not get that one exactly right.

After we left the church, we were heartbroken. After all, it was everything we had always wanted in a church, tons of wonderful people and wonderful friends, a great staff, and an awesome Pastor, who frequently moved my wife and I to tears.

After a few weeks of relief with no obligations, which by the way were thrown on someone else's obviously broader shoulders than mine, I began to feel at peace again and I began to hear God calling me back to church. We were visiting other churches and believe me I did not want to hear this call. Therefore, I stiff-armed and stiff-armed God, but he was not going away. Clearly, I knew God wanted me to return to the same church. Well let us just say my pride was about the size of a football field and I did not want to go back at first. It took a few days for me to work my pride out of the way. I would credit a lot of that work to a Brother in Christ who said to me at lunch one afternoon. "Troy, I am not going to let the growth problems at this church keep me away from worshiping God and fellowshipping with all the friends I have made."

In that moment, it hit me like a ton of bricks. In Ephesians 4:1-3, Paul tells us that:

"As a prisoner for the Lord then I urge you to live a life worthy of the calling you have received. Be completely humble and gentle, be patient, bearing with one another in love. Make every effort to keep the unity of the Spirit through the bond of peace." (NIV)

Yes and when it hit it hurt and I felt so silly. You see I had lost sight of my purpose. I am seeking to be like Christ, I am daily working through the process of sanctification. It is not about me, it is about God! The interesting thing is that I forgot what Paul teaches us to hear. Paul is telling us that transformation absolutely requires the presence of other people. Yes, he means to tell us that if we want to grow in Christ, if we want to be transformed and made new in our minds and our attitudes, then we must be engaged in sacrificial other people-centered relationships for transformation to occur. Look at what he is saying. We must do four things:

1) Be completely humble.
2) Be gentle.
3) Be patient.
4) And bear up with one another in love.

For every one of these commands we must have other people.

Back to the story.

I returned to church and was greeted with warm handshakes, smiles, and hugs. Within a week, everything was back to normal, and I was doing the same things I was before. Well guess what? Things were being stirred a little bit more in the kitchen. I was asked to take on more responsibility in leadership and finance roles and again I did so, without resolving the core truth that I was struggling with, the integrity of leadership! I plugged away for about six weeks and then everything came to a halt for me. I completely unplugged myself. Yes. I left again. This time it was for good! We would find a new church home and start over again. I blamed no one and still held everyone in high regard, but I had not resolved the personal conflicts I was having.

During some of the growth issues at the church, I had been introduced to the writings of Dietrich Bonhoeffer. Being completely intrigued by his writings, I studied them with a passion. Then I came across a passage that my Pastor had e-mailed me earlier in the year. Bonhoeffer says,

"People enter relationships with their own particular ideals and dreams of what community should look like. But God's grace quickly frustrates all such dreams. A great disillusionment with others, with Christians in general, and, if we are fortunate, with ourselves, is bound to overwhelm us as surely as God desires to lead us to an understanding of genuine Christian community. The sooner this moment of disillusionment comes over the individual and the community, the better for both. Those who love their dream of a Christian community more than the Christian community itself become destroyers of that Christian community even though their personal intentions may be ever so honest, earnest, and sacrificial."
— Dietrich Bonhoeffer

After studying this for a long time, I began to understand that I was this person. My dream of how the Christian community should be exceeded my passion for the community itself. That coupled with an overwhelming workload gave way to my final departure.

After we left that last time I was on my knees questioning God, his will for my life, and even his very existence. I did not understand the pain of separation I felt from his Church. I would liken it to the loss of my first love. I longed for God's Church when I was away from it; I ached to be a part of it. Still to this day, I often wonder what it was that I gave up by walking away and I will probably never know! My business then became understanding what it was that God wanted me to learn from this series of painful events. What I have uncovered in my soul searching has been all-powerful in my transformation process.

In my self-evaluation, I came to realize that I had two major flaws in my character that have always been a problem in my life. These are,

1) Expectations of others and myself — I allowed myself to trust heavily in others and I was let down often. I placed my own expectations and ideals on the performance of others and that was not right of me. Then I came across the Scripture in Psalms 118:8:

"It is better to take refuge in the Lord than to trust in man." (NIV)

What I have learned from this scripture is that I must put my expectations of others on the shelf and trust that God is working things out with his people in his way and not in mine. DO not get me wrong; I still trust my friends, but I do not place my expectations upon them. I cast them upon God and work through my issues with God. This is what the relationship is about. It is talking to God about the things that are troubling me.

2) My second huge character flaw -Acting on Emotions instead of faith — Well this one was not that hard as I had recalled all the trouble Moses had bringing the Israelites to the Promised Land. Moses was bombarded with trials, complaints, and troubles during his journey. They had been wandering in the desert for about thirty-eight years when they came to the Desert of Zin. It was here that Moses encountered a great problem. There was no water for the people or livestock. Moses fell to his knees and the Lord appeared before him and told him to speak to the rock and tell it to pour out its water in front of the people. In Numbers 20:10-11 Moses says:

"….Listen, you rebels, must we bring you water out of this rock? Then Moses raised his arm and struck the rock twice with his staff." (NIV)

What just took place here? Moses disobeyed God's command by striking the rock instead of speaking to it, and for that reason God forbade him to go into the Promised Land. The real question is, why did Moses strike the rock instead of speak to it, as God commanded? I am going out on a limb here, but after studying the passage, I would say that Moses was tired, frustrated, and angry with the people. Would you agree? Is that a fair assumption? Well, I would surmise that when Moses struck the rock, he did so in anger or unholy emotion. When he said, "Listen, you rebels," I am hearing anger. I am hearing emotion that says, "I am tired of you acting this way, so look at what I am doing for you. I am going to give you another miracle, water from a rock." In doing so, he gives the impression that it is his work, or his miracle, and not God's.

In a similar fashion, I somehow felt that God was calling me to leave the church because of some growth issues. I was saying that maybe my leaving would fix the problems by forcing the hand of others, instead of allowing God's timetable to do the work. I acted in unholy emotion instead of a steadfast trust in God.

Well, that is enough of that. Through chewing on the word, God revealed two areas of my life that needed transformation. I came to realize through self-evaluation that the reasons I left the church were that I have always placed high expectations on myself and other people and I have always had a tendency towards acting in unholy emotion rather than wisdom.

The gift here was this: As I began to discern my shortcomings, God began whispering in my ear. I was hearing, "Troy, I do not want to change them, I want you to change!"

Well, you might ask, where was my family in all this? They were right there beside me as always, but not happy about it. By now I was hearing almost daily, "Daddy can we go back to our old church, we miss it, please, pleeeeeaassseee!!!" My ever loving and supportive wife left me alone and let me work it out on my own, never putting pressure on me, but I knew she missed her friends. I had been crying out to God for direction and it finally came in the form of a plea from my wife and children to return to our old church. I reluctantly agreed because they had twice followed me. It was my turn to follow them.

Being armed with what I felt was an accurate self-appraisal and a willingness to learn from my character defects I faced my demons. I called my Pastor, I made amends where I needed to, and we returned to church, again. Most friends were great, welcoming, and warm. Some were angry, and rightly so. As the opportunities availed themselves, I approached each person I felt tension from and asked their forgiveness. Our family is attending church there again and we are slowly working ourselves back into the mix. This time I am, however, following my Godly principles. Again, in my life, even with a set of guidelines, it is very difficult for me to balance my life.

#6 Personal Time

Well, I am working on this area. Currently, I spend 45-50 minutes three days a week exercising. I read heavily at every opportunity I get. I read books about God, transformation, and such. I write about my life whenever I get the chance and I keep a regular journal. I love collecting DVD movies and watch them whenever I can find some free time. Finally, I love golf and aspire to play it more. I schedule in roughly an hour of free time every day. Sometimes I lay in bed and watch TBN, Storm Stories or the Discovery Channel and just rest. This is #6 in my schedule.

#7 God

Well, finally, you say! At the end of my day I go to God on my knees in prayer with a grateful heart and thank him for the day, for the good and the bad, ask his forgiveness, and I am quick to do an inventory of my day. If I have wronged someone, I make a note and correct it. Sometimes I will spend three minutes and sometimes I spend fifteen. It just depends on where I am in my journey that day.

So, what does your calendar look like? What are you going to put in your schedule to ensure that you become a man, woman, or child of God?

Developing Godly Self-Control

In Titus 2:11; Paul writes:

"For the grace of God that brings salvation has appeared to all men. It teaches us to say "No" to ungodliness and worldly passions, and to live self-controlled, upright and godly lives in this present age..."(NIV)

Godly Self-Control, defined, is:

" the ability to exercise restraint over one's own impulses, desires, words, emotions and personal direction."(NIV)

Godly self-control means that we use Godly discipline in our daily lives. It means we dismiss the temporary quick fix for the eternal crown. It means that we delay gratification of our flesh or earthly thinking so that we may have the gift of eternal life as our reward.

Godly self-control is not a picture of my family and I shopping on what we have come to joke about as impulsive Sunday. When we were younger in our faith, and we had some

112

money, and we wanted something, we bought it, without any forethought. We just did it. There was no thought as to the consequences of our actions; we simply acted on impulse to soothe our desire to have something. This is impulsive action. Godly discipline would require the exact opposite action, or the ability to say, "No, we did not budget for it, let's wait and see if we can afford it and we will come back later."

Self-control means that we have to get past that idea that the right-now quick fix is going to make us whole. We must dismiss the idea of the right now for the reward of the eternal crown. America generally is a quick fix nation. We have fast food, fast cars, fast computers, and fast cell phones, fast modems all created under the illusion that they will give us more free time. I do not know about you, but ever since computer stuff came out it seems as though I work more.

Happiness by definition is an occurrence; it is not a continual state of mind. Has anyone ever said, "Do you have happiness today, or I am full of happiness today." I hope not, it sounds a bit silly! We are generally happy over an occurrence or an event. Joy on the other hand could be defined as the confident assurance of God's love and work in our lives and the continued belief that he will always be. Therefore, would it be fair to say that happiness is based on an event or events, but joy is based on the promise that God in Christ Jesus provides. It is a state of mind. So if we choose to live out of joy, which is the fruit of the spirit, we can then begin the transformation process of letting go of the right-now quick fixes that we think make us happy, but mostly just cost us dollars and an expanding waistlines. We then focus on the thing that bring us joy, which is knowing God better.

Do you get the idea here; can you comprehend what is taking place out there? Everybody wants everything right now and I am just as guilty as the next. We have to quit eating, spending, and escaping to find peace. We have to go to God to find that missing peace.

Would you agree that a fair assumption for Godly self-control would be to tackle the most prominent and difficult problems in our lives right now, so that we can enjoy the reward of our eternal crown later?

OK, I hear you, but it is not that easy to say "NO" to such powerfully destructive feelings, to uncontrollable cravings for alcohol, drugs, food, and shopping, and to selfish bodily desires that we know are immoral.

Well, first, let us remember who we are now. We are a new creation, we are in Christ, we are justified, grace bestowed. We must learn how to plug into the power of God's grace and live out of that power. We do this by simply saying, "no" to the flesh or our old way of thinking and, "yes" to the word of God. In order to exercise this power, we have to have a sense of urgency about us. We need to be consumed with the idea that we must learn how to conquer the sinful nature that resides in us if we are going to grow. Here is how we do it.

A Personal Inventory

First, we take a personal inventory of ourselves and all of our known defects of character. We begin by reviewing the past thirty days in as much detail as we can painfully muster. On a sheet of paper, we make two sets of three t-bars, unless you are like me and need an extra page or two. In the first set of bars, in column one, we record the last known memory we have that would dictate a destructive habit or activity and we place a date beside it. These destructive habits would be similar to lusting, envy, gossip, pride, sloth, greed, expectations, acting on emotions, lying, stealing, or any other habit you or the Bible would view as a destructive lifestyle. In the second column, we

114

leave it blank until that defect arises again. When it does we place the date of the occurrence, and the third column we write down how we responded to the defect, how we felt etc. Once completed, we proceed to do the exact same thing but this time we record our cravings for food, spending, drinking, smoking, alcohol, or sex, etc. It is imperative that we thoroughly evaluate all the areas of our lives that cause us to place God in the passenger seat.

Second, once we have completed this uncomfortable task, we share it with God in prayer, and a spiritual partner if you wish. My prayer sounds like this:

Prayer
"God, thank you for helping me identify the things in my life that are keeping me from knowing you better and are causing me pain. I give these cravings and behaviors to you and pray that you would help me live out of the grace you have provided in me and turn from these sinful behaviors. Amen.

Third, we go about our daily lives and when our sinful nature arises we record it, then by the power of the Holy Spirit who resides in our hearts we command that sinful thought to flee and it will. Then we must journal of our experience. Remember, we are made in the image of God, we are a new creation, and God has placed in us a new heart and given us a fresh start. We have the power to repel Satan and his way of thinking. We have the presence of the Holy Spirit to guide us. Do not look at this process as self-denial. You are not denying yourself anything. What you are doing is allowing the power and grace of God to work through you and you are training your mind to rethink how it responds to its cravings. Soon enough you will be craving a relationship with God more than the cigarette you have been trying to give up for years.

Fourth: Since we have already set up our daily schedule in our calendar or outlook, it is imperative that we take this next step. Step four says that each week we should review our t-bars and we determine where we have given into our sinful nature and where we have been successful. We thoroughly evaluate our progress and determine where our weak spots are. We will be able to determine when our sinful nature strikes and why! Maybe it's the late afternoon and no one is at the office and you want a drink or a quick look at that website. Maybe your family is out and you have an opportunity to go chat with your neighbor who hangs out by the pool all day in her bikini. Maybe the kids have gone to school, your husband is at work and you break out the sweets. Whatever the case is, we are constructively identifying those things that bring us shame, guilt and self condemnation. Those things that disconnect us from God, those things that block us from the sunlight of the Spirit. The very things that will keep us swimming in our own lake of fire, filled with self contempt and self doubt.

We identify our weak spots and command the sinful thought to flee from us as Jesus did in Matthew 4:10;

"Away from me Satan!" (NIV)

Then we can proactively share our successes and failures with our spiritual friend. If we continue to have trouble in our weak areas, then we must arrange our schedules so that we are not alone or tempted. It is imperative that we have someone who can hold us accountable for our actions. A Brother or Sister in Christ who understands what it means to speak the truth in love.

Once we have completed this weekly review, we again kneel before God in gratitude for the progress we have made and ask for his wisdom and grace to overcome the trouble spots we are encountering.

Remember, when we were living in our sinful nature, our bodies told us what to do. Now that we are living out of our new nature, we are living by the spirit, which is Gods word, the truth and the Holy Spirit is guiding our thought life. Our bodies no longer drive our actions.

"Those who belong to Christ Jesus have crucified the sinful nature with its passions and desires. Since we live by the spirit let us keep in step with the spirit." (NIV)
Galatians 5:24-25

Paul gives us a snapshot of what it looks like to nail our old sinful nature to the Cross. However, you and I know that we will again see these demons rear their ugly heads, but now we are prepared to fight the earthly battle. Since we are blessed as God says we are, we will overcome many difficulties quickly. We will also be able to flush out our greatest weaknesses. This is the heart of the matter because Satan will continually tempt you where you are weakest. This process will help you prepare for battle. Hear Peters words in 1 Peter 2:11;

"Dear friends, I urge you, as aliens and strangers in the world, to abstain from sinful desires, which war against your soul."(NIV)

Make no mistake about it dear friends; our flesh is constantly at war with our spirit. Remember we are in the process of transformation and it lasts a lifetime. Renewing the mind and putting on the new is a daily occurrence. Most of my greater demons have been burning in Hades for a long time, but I still struggle with quite a few persistent ones.

Folks, please understand that this is not a self-help suggestion or ideal. This is a tool to help you manage and remove your defects one by one. This is done by tapping into the grace God has already given you in your new nature. The power is yours, Christ defeated the power of sin, Satan, and death on the Cross, and that power is ours, as we transform our lives and continue to develop a heart for Jesus.

Make no mistake about it, neither self-effort nor self-discipline will save us from our sins, Christ alone can do this. However, once we have accepted Christ as our Lord and Savior, begin to understand grace and are living out of that grace, the power to resist temptation is in our grasp. We must, however, recognize that our ability to walk away from our old nature requires a strong will, self-discipline and Godly motivation!

Developing a Spirit of Godly Motivation

"All a man's ways seem innocent to him, but motives are weighed by the Lord." (NIV)
                    Proverbs 16:2

When our foundation in life or our motivation is not firmly rooted in the scripture, our motives can be deceitful even to ourselves. Therefore, we must always evaluate our motives before we act and before we commence on any particular motivation. As Christians, our true north or our true motivation should be to develop a Heart for Jesus and desire to become just like Christ. Our true Godly motivation is fourfold. It should encompass:

A desire for accomplishment — It is based on the desire to accomplish the tasks that God set before us, to put off the old self, to renew our minds and our attitudes, to put on the new self, to bear up with one another in love, to be humble and patient and gentle with one another. Our motivation to live a life for Christ should, in itself, manifest its own natural desire to succeed. Why?

A desire to have - Because God wants us to Have and I desire to have the promises that God has set out for me in his

118

word. Things like an eternal life, prosperity, fruitfulness, wisdom, joy, love, understanding, and the list goes on. Our motivation to share in the riches of his sovereign grace should reign supreme in our lives. Why?

A desire to witness and testify, similar to the Acts of the Apostles - Because the gifts motivate us to Act on his instruction to share the gospel, to witness of our transformations and grace he has provided in our lives, to reach out and minister to others. To act in love and to give freely of what we have been given. It is the true motivation to become just like Jesus. It is the idea that, before we act on anything, we would ponder the question, "What would Jesus do if he were sitting beside me right now?" Why?

To desire to develop A heart for Jesus! We are called to reflect Gods glory. This is the goal that we as Christians must pursue. This is our goal as we walk through this incredibly foggy and terribly ambiguous existence of this place called earth. When our true north, our self-motivation, our Godly self-control and Godly discipline are all based on the ultimate purpose of our lives, that goal becomes attainable and we are ready to run the race. The final hurdle we will face will be developing Godly persistence.

Developing a Spirit of Godly Persistence

"Therefore since we are surrounded by such a great cloud of witnesses, let us throw off everything that hinders and the sin that so easily entangles and let us run with perseverance the race marked out for us. Let us fix our eyes on Jesus, the author and perfecter of our faith, who for the joy set before him endured the cross, scorning its shame and sat down at the right hand of the throne of God." (NIV)

Hebrews 12:1-2

OK, I do not know about you but this scripture moves me. It brings everything into perspective, because people who are asking questions surround us. They are asking, "Is this God thing real?" "What is it all about?" Brothers and Sisters in Christ who want to know, surround us! Therefore, we strive to balance our lives between who we say we are and how we live our lives. We must persevere through the trials this life has to offer and we must do it in such a way that we reflect Gods glory and his light will burn through us before man, that they may see God's good works. We must fix our eyes on the prize and never let go of the process by which we achieve that prize. When we are about to fall or we are tempted to fall, we must recall the pain Christ endured so that we could go free. We must, when tempted, desire to have A Heart for Jesus! This should be our goal!

Godly perseverance is:

"the patient endurance of hardship, a willingness to press on for the prize in spite of difficulties and extreme hardships."(NIV)

I have failed at many things in my life and I have made many wrong turns in my life but I refuse to quit searching. I have felt so alone and so distant from God at times that I would cry in my shower and scream at the top of my lungs, Abba, Father, I know you are there and I know you love me, and I will not stop seeking you no matter what!

I know you are just like me. You have all the Godly persistence you will ever need sitting right there in your heart. Tap the grace that God provides in Christ Jesus, light the fuse, ignite the power of Christ's victory at the Cross, believe in God with all your heart and all your soul and all your mind and he will meet you in the middle. Cry out to God as loud as you can when you hurt, let him know you are going to stay there until you get what you are praying for.

Persevering to develop a heart for Jesus will bring trails, I can promise you that. There is one roaming the earth that does not want you to reach your Godly goals, he wants you to think that you do not need God, that you can do it on your own, he wants you to believe that God is just an imaginary friend for grown ups. His name is Satan and we must go into this process of developing a heart for Jesus knowing that we will have to do battle with this demon. Satan will tempt you just as he tempted Eve in the garden, just as he tempted Jesus in the desert. He will lure you into his web; he will tell you all this can be yours if you just follow him.

We must be faithful, we must be persistent and above all, we must not fall into self-pity. When we are at our lowest, he will come calling and Satan will tempt us!

"I never saw a wild thing feel sorry for it itself. A frozen bird drops dead on the bow without ever having felt sorry for itself."
—D. H. Lawrence

Chapter 7 Study Guide

Q1: What is the most important race you will run?

Q2: Explain different behaviors that cause you problems and separate you from God.

Q3: How are you developing spiritually?

Q4: How do we discipline our hearts?

Q5: Share your thoughts on the 5 ideas of Godly discipline!

Q6: Is your love for others true or conditional? Site different instances.

Q7: How are you reflecting Gods glory?

Q8: Explain what it means to you to live by the Spirit!

Q9: Make a list of your priorities as they currently are ordered. After prayer and discussion with your group make adjustments as the Spirit would lead you.

Q10: In what areas of your life are you operating in the, "I don't know, I don't know area"

Q11: Write about your ministry work and how it affects you!

Q12: What is your understanding of Bonhoeffer's quote?

Q13: Do you have any character flaws that are causing you to stumble?

Q14: In what areas do you need more Godly self control?

Q15: In what areas do you need more Godly motivation?

Q16: In what areas do you need more Godly persistence?

Chapter 8

Who Will Tempt You?

OK, the goal is to develop a Heart for Jesus. We understand now that our transformation must be rooted in Gods word, the truth. We also know that in order to truly have a Heart for Jesus we must live a spiritual life, which is to say we must agree with Gods word in all we do to be rooted in the truth. The process of change is called sanctification. The roots of our transformation are founded in the power and grace we receive when we come to Christ. The process by transformation occurs is three fold (remember Ephesians):

- putting off the old nature
- renewing our minds
- putting on the new nature

We are now focused on the process of spiritual transformation through the development of other-centered sacrificial relationships and the development of Godly goals and disciplines. The Godly disciplines of goals, self- control, motivation, and endurance are the keys that help us unlock the doors to our sinful way of thinking. With these disciplines rooted firmly in our walk to develop a Heart for Jesus we will begin reaping the fruit of the Spirit. Where, in our innermost being we found loneliness, confusion and emptiness, we now find the Holy Spirit filling us with the peace of God. We are learning to walk in the Spirit of love and grace abounds in the garden of our hearts. The desire to fill our emptiness with stuff has been removed and in its place we have the gift of the Holy Spirit!

Great, but I am still having trouble, you say. Well, I anticipated that because I too still have trouble. I have found

124

something to be very true in my life. Hear this and hear it well! THE CLOSER WE GET TO GOD, THE HARDER SATAN WILL WORK ON US. I wish I could tell you the things he puts in my mind to convince me that I cannot write this book. Do not make the mistake of thinking that Satan is not real. You cannot believe just part of the Bible. Since you believe in God, since you believe in his word, you therefore must take all of his word to heart. Remember his word is truth! We live by his word and we live by the spirit. Satan is a part of that word and we are greatly cautioned throughout the Scriptures to guard our hearts and our minds from him. In 1 Peter 5:8-9, Peter warns:

"Be self-controlled and alert. Your enemy the devil prowls around like a roaring lion looking for someone to devour. Resist him, standing firm in the faith, because you know your brothers throughout the world are undergoing the same kind of sufferings." (NIV)

Peter is telling us that we must watch out for the devil at all times. We must cling to Christian relationships and walk through trials together. We must always focus on unity because it will be harder for the devil to attack us and succeed when we are with other Christians. I do not want to devote a lot of time to this because of his very nature, but if we are not aware of his power then we are operating our faith in that area we call, "What I don't know, that I don't know," and I believe we all agree that it is dangerous territory.

You see, Satan caused the fall of man, as we have discussed, and he, who was originally an angel of God, became corrupt through his own pride. Satan considers God his enemy and tries to limit his work in us. Here is the difficult part. God in his infinite wisdom has made us in his image and deep inside everyone of us God has placed a desire to know him. God calls us: God has given us a one up on Satan, however God in his sovereign love for us has also given us the freedom to choose

God over Satan. He has given us the freedom to choose good thoughts or bad thoughts. Worry or faith! The theme of the Book of Galatians is the gift of freedom. Paul tells us we are a new creation. We have freedom in Christ from the power of sin, death, and Satan. We are free to live out of the grace that God provides in Christ Jesus. God loves us enough to let us go. He realizes that the lustful desires of this world are mighty in their force. He knows the world where Satan lives is masked with ambiguities, falsehoods, thick blinding fog, lies, and deceit.

Well, the doubting Thomas asks, how do you know Satan lives here on Earth? I always thought he lived in hell. Great question! As a child, I was always taught the same thing. In Job 1:6-7:

"One day the angels came to present themselves before the Lord, and Satan also came with them. The Lord said to Satan, "Where have you come from?" Satan answered the Lord, "From roaming through the earth and going back and forth in it." (NIV)

You see I accept the Bible as Gods written word, every single part of it, not just what suits me! This is how I know Satan roams the earth, because the Bible said it. As if that were not enough, just look at the choices people make every day, look around you and you will know that the earth is where Satan roams; God knows that Satan is here to tempt us. God knows we are born of Adam, with a sinful nature. God knows we have a heart for sin. That is what makes the story of Jesus so powerful. For those very reasons, God is asking us as humans to put away everything that is our nature, everything that our hearts are inclined to, and freely choose to love God and not Satan. We are choosing a road that calls for the removal of the right now, feel-good pleasures of this earth in order that we may have an eternal crown. We are choosing to live out of God's power and grace while we are here on earth. We are choosing to give others a little taste of what Christ is like by being the salt and light to those who are lost in their sinful nature. After all, what is love if it cannot be freely chosen?

Who will tempt you? Satan will! When you are weak, when you are strong, when you are tired, when you are at rest, when you are happy, and when you are sad. There will always be an opportunity for Satan to tempt us. So how do we protect ourselves? First, we must believe he is real. Second, we must understand that Satan attacks us subtly in our thoughts, our dreams, our pride, and in our relationships. Yes friends, Satan finds fertile soil in our thought life. He attacks us in our thinking. Remember, the flesh is a way of thinking, just as the spirit is a way of thinking. We are either living by Gods word, which is truth, or the spirit or we are living by our word and our thoughts, which is the flesh. As we draw closer to God, what do we do to stop him? We must dress ourselves in the armor of God! Let's take a look at Ephesians 6:10-17:

"Finally be strong in the Lord and in his mighty power. Put on the full armor of God so that you can take your stand against the devil's schemes. For our struggle is not against flesh and blood, but against the rulers, against the authorities, against the powers of this dark world and against the spiritual forces of evil in the heavenly realms. Therefore put on the full armor of God, so that when the day of evil comes, you may be able to stand your ground, and after you have done everything to stand. Stand firm then, with the belt of truth buckled firmly around your waist, with the breastplate of righteousness in place, and with your feet fitted with the readiness that comes from the gospel of peace. In addition to all of this, take up the shield of faith, with which you can extinguish all the flaming arrows of the evil one. Take the helmet of salvation and the sword of the Spirit, which is the word of God, and pray in the Spirit on all occasions with all kinds of prayers and requests." (NIV)

Yes, Satan is an evil and deceitful fallen angel who has fooled most of the world into thinking that we are fighting flesh and blood. No, it is not one another that we fight. It is Satan and his legion of fallen angels who seek to destroy God's Church. Our defense is to dress ourselves in the armor of God. We must strive to develop a heart for Jesus. Our offense is to carry a torch of light that burns brightly in our hearts, that lights our path, so that even in the darkest hours of people's lives, they may see the good works of our Father who is in Heaven, and they too will ache to have a heart for Jesus. We will, one by one, bring each and every heart to the Lord by balancing our lives between who we say we are and how we live our lives. We will build the Church into a place where every man, every woman, and every child will see the character and integrity that burns from the pulpit and the ministries the congregations provide.

Do you remember when Moses returned from the mountain? Do you remember that his face burned so brightly with the glory of God that the Israelites could not look at him? I do and it so inspires me to know God better. My heart aches for the kind of leadership that will move our world closer to Gods word and farther from our sinful flesh. We will wage the spiritual war against Satan and his legion of fallen angels by saying "NO" to the sinful nature and "Yes" to Jesus. We will make the salt tastier than it has ever been and we will make the light burn brighter than ever before as we grow our hearts for Jesus.

So carry on in your faith, dear people, and when the murkiness, gloom, and thick blinding fog role into your life, when the clouds thicken and begin to penetrate your shield of faith, remember what Jesus told Peter in Matthew 16:18:

"On this rock I will build my church and the gates of Hades will not overcome it." (NIV)

Hear the words of our Lord Jesus Christ in John 6:37-39;

"All that the Father gives me will come to me and whoever comes to me I will never drive away. For I have come down from heaven not to do my will but to do the will of him who sent me. And this is the will of him who sent me, that I shall lose none of all that he has given me, but raise them up on the last day." (NIV)

WOW! What a promise! Friends, if you have ears to hear, then hear these words, Jesus is telling us that it is Gods will that we come to Jesus and that once we do Jesus will not lose one of us. Ok, I did not get it a first either. After chewing on it I started thinking about how I feel when I fail and give into sin. I feel like I have been conquered by Satan, then I started traveling down that road of guilt and self condemnation, but hear Jesus' words hear. He will not lose one of us who has come to him! Jesus is telling us that he is with us, while we are in this world, he knows we will fall, but he will help us back up again, he will raise us up above our sinful ways and lift us to glory, if we only come to him! Jesus is also telling us that this is his Fathers will and that he places his Fathers will above his own. Jesus is setting the bar for us, if you will. He is telling us that it is more important for him to do his Fathers will not his own. What does that mean? Let me translate; if we are to walk with Christ then we must put the will of God ahead of our will, Gods way ahead of our way, we must emulate the work of Jesus to suffer his human emotions for the sake of our salvation.

So let us not be deceived by Satan's tempting ways, but let us be encouraged by the word of God and let us grab hold of the keys that will unlock the door to victory!

Chapter 8 Study Guide

Q1: Explain the importance of other centered relationships and how they keep you focused?

Q2: List the different ways Satan tempts you!

Q3: Are you a positive or negative thinker?

Q4: Describe what happens to you when Satan tempts you thru your thought life!

Q5: Explain how you use the armor of God to battle your sinful nature!

Chapter 9

Five Keys to Victory

"To be blind is bad, but worse is to have eyes and not see."
— Helen Keller

KEY #1-A Believing Heart!

The number one key to Victory is going to be your heart. Do you truly believe with all of your heart in God's promise in Christ Jesus? Do you truly believe that transformation is for you? Are you still reading and doubting?

Well, I must admit that there was a time, too, when I felt just as you may right now, if you are dealing with some of the issues I have dealt with in my life. Is there still a wall that separates your mind from your heart? Is your heart aching for the change but your mind just will not let you believe? The Bible has an explanation for that! His name was Thomas and he was a disciple. Have you ever heard the phrase "doubting Thomas?" I have and I was a doubter, too. Then I reread the story in John, when Thomas, one of the twelve disciples, refused to believe that Jesus had rose from the dead, and he said in John 20:25:

"...unless I see the nail marks in his hands and put my finger where the nails were, and put my hand into his side, I will not believe it." (NIV)

The Bible says that about a week later Jesus appeared to the disciples again. In John 20:27-29, Jesus said to Thomas:

"Put your finger here; see my hands. Reach out your hand and put it in my side. Stop doubting and believe. Thomas said to him, "My lord, my God!" Then Jesus told him, "Because you have seen me you have believed; blessed are those who have not seen and yet believe." (NIV)

The idea here is that we have the freedom to doubt or the freedom to believe. Choose, right now, to believe with all your heart, your entire mind, and all your soul that God can deliver you from your sinful nature and through God's grace, your life will be transformed. Say it, profess it, and shout it aloud. "God, I believe you can save me, I believe you will do what you say you will, Abba, Father, I believe you with all of my heart, my soul and my mind."

Key #2 –Spoken Faith

I believe this with all my heart! If I believe in something, then speak about it, it usually happens! If I believe I will succeed because God said I would, I speak about how I will succeed, then in The spirit of faith I will succeed.! The second Key to Victory is to actually say it. Let your mind be ruled by your new heart for Jesus. Let your body and your mind hear your confidence, your newfound unwavering faith in the truth. Cry out to your Father in Heaven, "I love you, Father, I believe you, Father. Open the door to Victory with the key of spoken faith!

You see, if you believe it in your heart, and you speak it with your voice, it is going to happen! What, you don't believe me? I can accept that; let us see what the Bible says about it.

Do you remember Peter, the rock, the one in which Christ would build his Church? Let's take a look in Matthew 16:13-19; where Jesus asks the disciples,

"Who do people say the son of man is?" They replied, "some say John the Baptist; other say Elijah; and still others, Jeremiah or one of the prophets." "But what about you?" Jesus asked. "Who do you say that I am." Simon Peter answered, "You are the Christ, the Son of the living God."" (NIV)

Let us look at what really happened here. Jesus was talking to all the disciples, but only Peter responded in faith. Only Peter spoke out and said what he believed in his heart. Peter believed with all his heart, soul, and mind that Jesus was Christ, the Son of the living God, and he spoke it. He believed it, he said it, it has certainly happened. Peter's profession of faith above all the other disciples set him apart. He became the role model for every single one of us. In order to know God personally, in order to be able to freely come to God, we must profess our faith in the living Christ. Thus, Peter, is the rock. He professed his faith in Jesus and became the model by which every one of us who comes to Christ must follow.

Peter believed it and he spoke it, and look what happened in Matthew 16:17-19:

"Jesus replied. "Blessed are you, Simon son of Jonah, for this was not revealed to you by man, but by my Father in heaven. And I tell you that you are Peter and on this rock I will build my church, and the gates of Hades will not overcome it. I will give you the keys to the kingdom of heaven; whatever you bind on earth shall be bound in heaven, and whatever you loose on earth will be loosed in heaven." (NIV)

Now I want to be very specific here. I have read many arguments for and against the meaning of this particular scripture and I understand through chewing on the word that it has been a subject for great debate. I do not have any purpose in that debate. I have a singular belief that keys are quite simply the tools that we need, as humans with a sinful nature, to open the doors that are blocking us from the sunlight of the spirit of Christ Jesus. Yes, these keys are the keys that we need to unlock the doors that are blocking us from transformation.

Yes, these keys unlock the power of the Cross in our hearts. These keys break through the doors of addiction, hate, lust, fear, pride, envy, sloth, and gluttony. These keys give us the power to say "yes" to Christ Jesus and "no" to our sinful nature.

Do you see? Do you hear what I am saying? We do not have to drink alcoholically anymore! We do not have to keep taking those prescription painkillers anymore! We do not have to live in fear anymore! We do not have to be chained to our eating disorder anymore! We do not have to keep smoking those cigarettes anymore! We do not have to gossip about our neighbors anymore! We do not have to keep up with the Joneses anymore! Through Christ Jesus, we have the power and the keys to unlock any door we need to in our lives.

Well, as if Peter was not enough, let us look at some other supporting scriptures.

A Spirit of Fear

Have you ever had a spirit of fear? I know I have and it still attacks me quite often. Fortunately for me, I know what to do with it. What really is a spirit of fear? Would it be fair to say that it is fear of the enemy, Satan, and what he can do to us? If so, then would it not be fair to say that the enemies Satan uses against us are worry, doubt, lust, discontentment, jealousy, bad relationships, greed, distrust, lawsuits, and on and on? Do these things not breed a spirit of fear into our lives? Remember where Satan gets us, that is correct, our thought life!

Since these things are true in my life, I am going to assume that some of you are like me! When the spirit of fear descends upon me, I have a choice. Either I can pray over it and

134

command it to flee from me or I can dwell on it. For a better part of my life, I did not have a heart for Jesus or the keys and the power to command it to flee, so I nurtured these fears. I rolled them around and around in my head like a little lead ball in a pinball machine. I would bounce around all types of fearful scenarios until, ultimately, if I carried them long enough I would do the unthinkable, I would speak of them.

Not too long ago I had a very lucrative business account. In fact, it was such a good account that I feared I would lose it. In fact, I spent so much time worrying about how I was going to keep the account that I began to fear losing it. Then I began to operate out of that fear and I nurtured that fear of losing that account. Then, a few months later I did the unthinkable, I spoke of the fears that I had come to believe in and, guess what? Yes, it happened, I lost the account!

I was dumbfounded; I could not believe that it had actually happened. Then I started reflecting on my life since I have been saved and I can count countless times where I have repeated the same behavior with positive and negative things in my life.

About a year into my walk with Christ, I was preparing to take a huge exam to get my landscape contractor's license. It was a big event for me as I was starting a new life, a new business, and was newly married with a child on the way. I have never been good at taking tests and was fearful. I remember deciding that I was not going to dwell on the fear but, to the contrary, was going to focus on success. Every day when I studied, I would pray to God for wisdom and then I would visualize what my success would look like. What would it feel like when I opened the letter and saw the passing mark? I envisioned elation, happiness, a celebration, the joy the accomplishment would bring my family, and the probable prosperity it would bring to our business. Then I would speak of it aloud to God. I would say to God in prayer, out loud, "Yes, we are going to do it together, we are going to pass this test." Then I would get to the business of studying. Well guess what? The test was impossible, but yes, I passed it! Do you know why? Because I believed in my heart, I spoke it, and it happened.

I had a similar experience with quitting smoking. For years, I tried to quit but failed miserably. I was always relying on the patch, gum, or something to get me through. Finally, one day I prayed hard about it, commanded the demon of nicotine to flee, then asked God for his help and visualized what success looked like. Then, I spoke aloud that I would succeed and guess what? It happened. I have not had a cigarette in over seven years.

I could literally go on and on with different examples in my life but I think you will understand better if we use some more scriptural examples.

Deuteronomy 28:7, says:

"The Lord shall cause thine enemies that rise up against thee to be smitten before thy face, they will come out against thee in one way, but flee from you in seven ways." (NIV)

I believe we all can conclude that the one way our enemy rises up against us is through the spirit of fear. Yes, Satan attacks our thought life or our flesh. Where did that fear come from? Remember Adam, in the Garden of Eden, we talked about earlier. Remember what Adam said in Genesis 3:9, when he responded to God:

"I heard you in the garden and I was afraid, because I was naked, so I hid." (NIV)

Thanks, Adam! Adam was the first to experience the spirit of fear and then he spoke of it when he said, "I was afraid."

Then we see Job speak of the spirit of fear in Job 3:25:

"What I feared has come upon me, what I dreaded has happened to me." (NIV)

The very things that Job feared the most he lost. The spirit of fear worked through him as well.

Then we see David in Psalm 116:10-11:

"I believed; therefore I said," I am greatly afflicted." And in my dismay I said, "all men are liars." (NIV)

We have witnessed the spirit of fear at work in Adam and Job and now we see David expound on the process of how it works. David believed all men were liars because of his circumstances. He had been hiding out in a cave for a long time because everybody, including his son, was trying to kill him. Follow the verse, David said, I believed, therefore I spoke it, and it happened, he was greatly afflicted.

Behold, there is excellent news here. Here is the key that unlocks the spirit of fear. This key blows the hinges off the door. Let us look at 2 Corinthians 4:13, where Paul gives us the key. He says:

"It is written:" I believed; therefore I have spoken." With the same spirit of faith we also believe and therefore speak," (NIV)

Therefore, we learn that just as the spirit of fear descends upon us we now have the key to renew our attitude and put on the spirit of faith. Yes, in Christ, you have the power.

So know you have the second key, if you believe it and you speak it, it will happen in the spirit of faith. In order to grow our spirit of faith it is urgent that we get to know him better. So how do we get to know him better? We seek him!

KEY #3 – Seek God Now!

The prophet Isaiah gives all of us Godly counsel in Isaiah 55: 6-11, as he speaks to the people of Israel:

"Seek the Lord while he may be found, call upon him while he is near. Let the wicked man forsake his way and the evil man his thoughts. Let him turn to the Lord and he will have mercy on him, and to our God for he will freely pardon. For my thoughts are not your thoughts neither are your ways my ways, declares the Lord. As the heavens are higher than the earth, so are my ways higher than your ways and my thoughts than your thoughts. As the rain and snow come down from heaven and do not return to it without watering the earth and making it bud and flourish, so that it yields seed for the sower and bread for the eater, so is my word that goes out from my mouth: It will not return to me empty, but will accomplish what I desire and achieve the purpose for which I sent it." (NIV)

Why is this a key to spiritual transformation? Because it is rooted in the truth, Gods word. Remember, if we want to get to the fruit of the thing then we have to dig deep inside us and remove the dirt that is covering our roots. Remember John 15:1;

"I am the true vine and my Father is the gardener." (NIV)

Therefore, would it be fair to say that Jesus is the vine, God is the gardener, and you and I are the branches. So God is the gardener responsible for removing unproductive branches or branches of the vine that are not fruitful, then who is responsible to ensure that we are remaining fruitful? Right! It is our individual responsibility to ensure that we are fruitful, as well as it is our responsibility to reach out and help others so that we can build up the vine, or the unity of the faith, Jesus' Church!

Are you with me? Good! It is our responsibility to produce good fruit, so I would ask you several questions.

1) What is Godly and what is not and how can we know?
2) What is righteous, what is not, and how can we know?

You see, the Lord tells us that our ways are not his ways; neither are our thoughts his thoughts. Man, this thing keeps getting harder. NO! That is precisely the point. We must seek him! Do you know we can follow the scriptures to understand the keys to a successful transformation? Isaiah is telling us to seek the Lord while he may be found, he is telling us that now is the time. It has a sense that it is urgent, we must not delay, we need to seek God now before it is too late.

OK, what does it mean to seek him? Well, it means we must seek to know and understand God's will and way for our life. We must come to know him better. We must hunger for knowledge of God. We need to meditate upon his word so that we would have a better understanding of who we are and what our job is with the time we have on this earth. Remember Gods word is truth, if we are seeking truth then we are seeking God and we are living by the Holy Spirit.

Where do we seek him? We start at church. That is just the tip of the iceberg. We must get into his word. We need to methodically study the scriptures to know him better. Remember our calendar; we are to schedule time in our day to study his word.

Why do we do this? Because Isaiah tells us that God's word shall accomplish the purpose for which he sent it. What is that purpose? That his word would not return to him empty. How do we accomplish that? Together, remember Ephesians 4:3-6:

"Make every effort to keep the unity of the spirit through the bond of peace. There is one body and one spirit—just as you were called to one hope when you were called—one Lord, one faith, one baptism; one God and Father of all, who is over all and through all and in all." (NIV)

We are all a part of the same body, we are all branches of the same vine, and we are all called to work together to build up the body of Christ's Church. We do this by spreading the Gospel, by ministering, by serving, through testimony, through sharing our faith, through evangelism, through seeking to understand his word so that we can share it with others, and thus it will not return to him empty but in fact will accomplish the purpose for which he sent it. A point of caution! Please do not get discouraged if you do not find him. The scripture did not say you would find him, it said seek him. Thanks Sandy!

OK, I am really beginning to understand, but what if I get uncomfortable? What if I get stuck in fear? Then cry out to God with all the strength you can muster!

KEY #4 - Cry out to God, Abba, Father, I need you!

If you have children, then I know you will quickly grasp this key. Think of the last time your child cried. My children have two cries. The first cry is a cry for sympathy or attention, more of a whiney cry when they cannot have their way. For example, when my son wants candy or my daughter wants money, or when one of my children wants to get the other one in trouble. It is a fake cry that we all can relate to as parents. OK, how do you respond to that kind of silliness? I don't know about you but I tell my kids that if they do not get along with each other that they are going to have to kiss and make up and spend an hour talking to each other nicely, without any other form of entertainment. That pretty much gets them in line!

Then there is that second kind of cry. It is that piercing wail of agony that streams forth from your child's heart that says, "Daddy!! Daddy!!!! Help me!!" Instantaneously you drop what you are doing and you go running to your children to help them, and you hold them and hug them and squeeze them and cry with them and buy them a prize and love them until they are OK to go out on their own again.

I can remember one of the hardest things I had been through in my life was watching my son get stitches in his forehead, right next to his eye. It happened about three years ago, the night before we were getting ready to leave for Disney World. We were all excited and Jackson and Wesleigh were horsing around. As they came running into the bathroom Jackson fell, hit his head on the tile steps of the bathtub and split his forehead wide open. Blood poured everywhere and his wails of pain beckoned us to his side. The worst was yet to come. Within fifteen minutes, he had calmed down and we were able to see the depth of the cut and decided to take him to the hospital. It was a long wait and he was up and running around in the waiting room before we knew it. They finally called us and off we went to get it looked at. The next thing I knew the doctor was sticking the tip of his finger in Jackson's head and Jackson was howling in pain. Don't you know that I just wanted to reach out and heal him, I wanted so badly to fix it that I cried out to God to take his pain away! I asked God to give it to me, I would take his pain, just please do not let him hurt anymore. As the pain got worse, they had to strap Jackson down in some thing they called a papoose so that they could finish stitching him up!

Wow! Don't you know how great the love for our children is? Don't you know what his mother and I would have done to ease his pain?

How much more do you think God wants to ease our pain? How much greater do you think God's love is for his children? Do not be afraid to cry out to God from the top of your lungs. Go into your room, get in your car, just cry out to him. Don't you know that God will come running when we truly cry out to him!! Do not just sit there and say, "If this is God's will, it will happen." Cry out to him, let him know your faith, let him know you're standing there, waiting for him to do what he has promised! If you doubt, read on to see what Paul says about it in Romans 8:12-16:

"Therefore, brothers, we have an obligation — but it is not to the sinful nature, to live according to it. For if you live according to the sinful nature, you will die; but if by the Spirit you put to death the misdeeds of the body, you will live, because those who are lead by the Spirit of God are sons of God. For you did not receive a spirit that makes you a slave again to fear, but you received the Spirit of sonship. And by him we cry, "Abba, Father." The spirit himself testifies with our spirit that we are God's children." (NIV)

Paul explains to us that if we are truly trying to renew our minds, if we are truly in Christ then we are truly "sons of God." Paul is telling us we are no longer slaves to our flesh but we are God's children and he encourages us to ask him for whatever we need! Abba, is the Aramaic word for father. We see Christ call out to his Father in the Garden. In Mark 14:36, Jesus cries out:

"Abba, Father, he said, everything is possible for you. Take this cup from me. Yet not what I will, but what you will." (NIV)

142

Even though Jesus' cup was much greater than anyone could ever possibly imagine, Jesus Christ, God's chosen son suffered alienation from his Father so that we may go free in our sins. This is the true love of our Father, God! Don't you believe that when we need him, he will come running! Moreover, remember, when God has comforted us and carried us through our trials, we must remember to use our final key to open the door of trust.

Key # 5 - Trust and do not be afraid!

As we grow in our transformation, God will call on us to do his bidding. You will feel his promptings in many ways. God has woken me up in the middle of the night for months about writing this book. I wake up with thoughts, I go to bed with thoughts, and I have had dreams of it. For many years, God has placed a vision before me of sharing the miracles of transformation he has performed in my life. I must say I have been fearful to let you know who I am. Honestly though, the call has become so incredibly strong that my faith far outweighs my fear about how this book will be received. You see, I believe God has called me to reflect his glory by sharing the miracles of transformation that he has manifested in my life. Remember, I cannot concern myself with how you will receive me, I need only be concerned with doing Gods will and walking in faith. I must put forth the footwork that will reflect God glory and grace and hopefully help others find a heart for Jesus.

Why do I share this? Because I want you to be prepared for your calling. If you honestly seek God, I know you will find the spirit of transformation and when you do it will change your life! You will begin to think differently, feel differently, and act differently. You will hunger for knowledge of him, you will hunger for change in your attitudes, you will see your problems in a new light, and you will be asked to do things that make you move out of your comfort zone. That is why the last key is trust. In Psalm 56: 3-4, David shares his trust in times of fear:

"When I am afraid, I will trust in you. In God, whose word I praise, In God I trust; I will not be afraid. What can mortal man do to me?" (NIV)

After all what do most of us fear more than anything, when it comes to stepping out in faith? I do not know about you, but the fear of failure and the fear of man and what he thinks can stop me dead in my tracks. Truly, what can mortal man do to me? He cannot do anything to me that I have not already done to myself! So trust in the Lord with all your heart, step out in faith, share God's grace in your life, take the sword of the spirit into everything you do, light up every room you walk into, bring the flavor of joy to your family and friends.

As you grow in your walk and begin to hear a calling on your life to serve, be sure to align your calling with your spiritual gifts. Most churches offer a class to evaluate what your gifts are. Let us take a brief glance at spiritual gifts.

Chapter 9 Study Guide

Q1: Are you a doubting Thomas? If so, How?

Q2: Do you have a believing heart now? In not, what is holding you back?

Q3: Describe some instance where you have thought and spoke your way into fortune or misfortune!

Q4: How are you seeking God?

Q5: Do you feel comfortable crying out to God? Please explain.

Q6: Are you ready to trust and not be afraid?

Chapter 10

Spiritual Gifts

In my walk with Christ, I have often devalued the person that I am. For many years, I tried the walk of a moralist, as we discussed earlier. Then I journeyed down the road of rewards for good behavior, all the time thinking that if I just keep living right and doing good deeds then God will love me. On the other hand, if I can just keep this law and 200,000 other laws I had placed upon myself, maybe God will love me. Needles to say, both ideas are biblically unfounded and entirely false. It is not a wonder that I felt like a failure so often in my walk to develop a heart for Jesus.

My biggest problem was that I suffered from spiritual ignorance. I was all over the place in my thought process. At first I thought Christianity was about how to have a good life, how to be a good person, how to be successful in my work. How to have happy kids and make money.

Well I have learned many things in my journey of sanctification. I have learned that Christianity is not about how to have a great life; Christianity is about a relationship with Jesus! It means going into training to become like Christ. It means keeping our eyes on the prize while we perform the hard work of crucifying the flesh; it means Godly self-control, Godly discipline, and Godly motivation. It means self-denial, it means looking in the mirror and getting to the root of who we are. It means finding out the truth about us. During this process of sanctification, we put on the new clothing of our new nature and we learn how to serve.

As we begin to feel the call to serve, we must look at what our spiritual gifts are. If you have not already done so at this point, it would be paramount for you to get involved with a spiritual gift class at your church. You will find a sense of belonging when your gifts are matched with ministry. Once you tie in with ministry then you begin to really get a feel for what it means to have sacrificial people-centered relationships. You build one another up, you help out when someone needs it, you form support groups, you fill in when someone is sick, you help other groups do missions, you have cookouts together, and pretty soon you have a brand new family.

However, if you do not know what your gifts are and you get involved in areas that do not bring you joy, you could create strife and discord without intent, and this would not build the unity of the Spirit.

So let's take a look at what Paul says about spiritual gifts in Ephesians 4:7-8. Paul tells us:

"But to each one of us grace has been given as Christ apportioned it, this is why it says, When he ascended on high he led captives in his train and gave gifts to men. What does "he ascended" mean except that he also descended to the lower, earthly regions? He who descended is the very one who ascended higher than all the heavens, in order that he may fill the whole universe." (NIV)

Do you enjoy the stories of Jesus as much as I do? How about the movies? Well, I have read about every story of Jesus' life I can get my hands on, watched every movie, and nothing every really seems to tackle the idea of what Paul is touching on here. After going through Matthew, Mark, Luke, and John several times, I began to get frustrated that my memory was accurate. I could not find any scripture about what took place between the time Jesus died on the Cross and his resurrection three days later. All four Gospels go from the death to the placement of his body at the tomb to the resurrection, each having its different peculiarities, which are not a subject of this discussion. Being overly intrigued, I began to research it.

Therefore, what did Jesus do in that time? Well, I began to chase the scriptures through the footnotes and references. And please understand that I am not trained in theology, but I believe I have a good picture of what took place here. However, I must state that I have been diligent for many, many years about seeking to understand God's word.

You may remember the old Nicene Creed where it says, "He descended into hell and on the third day he arose from the dead and ascended into heaven." In hell, or Hades, as I understand it, was the home of the sinful dead and the home of the righteous or paradise. This is where all the Old Testament saints and souls are at rest. They are awaiting the promised Messiah. Some also believe that it is the resting place of our souls between the time of death and resurrection, when Christ returns again. So the home of the righteous or paradise is where all the saints dwelled, who had lived Godly lives, before Calvary. They were awaiting the arrival of the promised Messiah. Remember what Jesus said to the thief on the Cross in Luke 23:43:

"Jesus answered him, "I tell you the truth, today you will be with me in paradise." (NIV)

Since Jesus' work on the Cross had not actually been completed, the thief would actually go to paradise. When Jesus died, he went to Hades for two reasons. In 1 Peter 3:18-20, Peter says:

"He was put to death in the body but made alive in the spirit through whom also he went and preached to the spirits in prison who disobeyed long ago when God waited patiently in the days of Noah." (NIV)

Reason #1 was that Christ went to Hades to declare his final victory to those imprisoned there for eternity. Then we see in 1 Peter 4:6, Peter says:

"For this is the reason the Gospel was preached even to those who are now dead..." (NIV)

Reason #2 was Jesus descended to go to the house of the righteous, or Paradise, and proclaim his Victory. To ensure the saints of Old Testament times that he was indeed the Messiah and that his work was complete.

"When you ascended on high you led captives in your train." (NIV) When Jesus ascended into Heaven, he brought with him all the souls who had been awaiting him along with the spoils of his Victory.

To paint a picture of what really happened on the Cross, we must understand what Jesus' mission was. Jesus' life was set out before him. Since Adam, God could not accept man as righteous in his eyes. Throughout the Old Testament, the only way to God was through a sacrifice. God's plan was to create the perfect sacrifice for the sin of mankind. God's design for Jesus' life was to be the conquering victor over sin, Satan, and death. So this is the Victory that takes place on the Cross. As Jesus ascended into Heaven, he took with him the spoils of Victory.

It is the idea that, in early times, when a conquering country would win a battle, its soldiers would return to their homes with a train of captives behind them. The spoils of victory would follow the soldiers, from riches to animals and even the prisoners. As the victors approached the city, they would give gifts to the people.

In the same way, Paul is using this picture to demonstrate that Christ, in his crucifixion and resurrection, was a conquering victor over sin, Satan, and death, and when Christ ascended into Heaven, he gave gifts to his Church. These gifts are further explained in Ephesians 4:11-13 when Paul tells us:

"It was he who gave some to be apostles, some to be evangelists, and some to be pastors and teachers, to prepare God's people for the works of service, so that the body of Christ may be built up until we all reach unity in the faith and in the knowledge of the Son of God and become mature attaining to the whole measure of the fullness of Christ." (NIV)

What is Paul talking about here? He is saying that the Holy Spirit has given each Christian special gifts for the building up of the Church. Whether you are called to evangelism, pastoring, teaching, administration, missions, or any type of ministry, your goal must be to seek out your spiritual gifts and exercise those gifts for the "works of service." We do these works of service so that we may grow in Christ, through the practice of serving others.

The purpose Paul describes is to prepare or equip God's people to do his work so that we may all reach the unity or oneness in our faith and through these works of service we will begin the transformation from the old self. We will commence to think, act, and respond more and more like Jesus. We will, in essence, be maturing in our faith through the works of service.

Therefore, we have a picture of spiritual gifts and why it is paramount that we find out what our gifts are. Once we acquire some knowledge through a church class about our gifts, it is imperative that we put them to use in our appropriate area of giftedness.

Many years ago that I took a spiritual gifts class. Up until then I had tried every single way I possibly could to get God to love me more. I never really felt worthy of serving God and I never really felt that I had anything to offer him in the way of service. I mean what could a recovering, 250-pound landscape contractor with a bad back do in the way of service work.

Folks, you have to understand this. My attitude was all wrong! I was spiritually ignorant of how God viewed me. I went to church, I tithed, I did a little service work when needed, but it was like pulling teeth. I read my Bible every day but it was more of a race to see how fast I could get through it than an actual journey into understanding. I mean I heard some of the things they were saying at church. I heard some of the things I was reading in the Bible and I was living a lot of my life right.

The problem for me was I was still searching for that missing "peace." Yea, I have had lots of success in business and a long relationship with God, but all along, I knew there was something missing. I know now that this is why my wife and I kept searching for another church where we could fit in.

Well, I want you to know that the best thing that ever happened to me at church was attending the Spiritual Gifts class. When I finished that course, I walked out of there a new man with an overwhelming hunger to serve God. You see, before I went into that class, I knew I was good at certain things but I had no idea how they could benefit the church. The greatest gift I received from the spiritual gifts class was the confident assurance that I had the ability to give back to God. I learned that I was worthy to serve him, that I could have an impact on the purpose for which God sent his word. Yes, I could ensure that his word would accomplish the purpose for which he sent it. I could be a part of ensuring that his word would not return to him empty!

Friends, understanding the fact that God could use me in his service has propelled me into a new dimension in my life. For close to four years now I have spent hours upon hours and

151

days upon days in sheer joy, chasing scripture, seeking knowledge of God, reading essays, books, and understanding who I am. Yes, understanding who I am, through knowing God better, has become one of the greater joys in my life. You, too, have spiritual gifts. Seek them now!

Chapter 10 Study Guide

Q1: Do you see yourself as a willing servant with gifts to use for works of service?

Q2: Do you feel called to serve in your church? If so where?

Q3: If offered will you take a spiritual gifts class?

Q4:If the gifts you have a different than where you thought will you serve where you want to or where god is calling you?

Q5: Explain how this book has helped you understand and develop a true heart for Jesus!

Chapter 11

Values

Spiritual gifts, works of service, sanctification, God centered living, persevering against our sinful nature, striving to understand who we are in Christ, are you serious, why all the work, I could just live the way I want to, doing what I want to and not have to deal with all this. Sure, we could say no to God and yes to the desires of our flesh could we not? Here is the problem with this! If you have come this far there really is no turning back. If you are here and you are making a sincere effort to grow in Christ then the Holy Spirit already has you. Truly, I can think of no other pain as great as grieving the Holy Spirit in my life now. Sin is no longer fun any more. When I fall, it is awful and I grieve the Holy Spirit. Have you noticed lately that you want to do certain things but for some reason it just does not feel right anymore. Have you noticed that you cannot just sit on the sidelines anymore? Have you noticed that when you are tempted there is a battle taking place? I sure have!

The Holy Spirit has entered your heart and he is guiding you. A prolific sense of right and wrong, sinful and Godly, action and inactivity are part of your values now. Yes, whether you realize it or not you are developing a Heart for Jesus and your heart hungers to live a Godly life. Peace should be ever present in your walk. Even in your trials, the Holy comforter is soothing you and protecting your heart from the evil one who attacks you in your thought life. As your journey has progressed over the pages of this book, you will have begun to ask yourself some significant questions that will continually paw at your heart until you begin to seek the answers. Why am I here? What am I living for? Where am I headed?

As a child I played games, hunted crawdads in creek beds, played cowboys and Indians with my friends, rode bikes and climbed trees. As a child, I lived for the moment! As a teenager I was lost in other peoples opinions of me and acted on what I thought would make me look good in your eyes. As a teenager, I lived for your approval! As a college student and young adult, I lived by impulse and desire and I ended up at deaths door, filled with shame, discontentment and self-loathing. Yes, as a college student and a young adult I cared not for anyone's approval because I had learned not to care about myself! As a Christian striving to live a life worthy of the calling I have received, I live with peace, gratitude, humility and a very close friend in Jesus. Today I value Gods word, the truth, a spirit filled life, and a yearning to have a Heart for Jesus.

My journey has taken me places I hope you never have to go, but if you do journey as far off Gods path as I have, Jesus will be their waiting for you to return to him!

So, what are your values in this life? Do you live your life effortlessly repeating the same silly things day in and day out with no real objective? Have you worked enough yet to stop and ask yourself what it is that you are working for? Have you been so put out with life and the God thing that you are wondering why you are here and what your purpose is? Friends, live your life with A Heart for Jesus and I will promise you these things as they have come true in my life! You will begin to understand that you are living for Jesus and for an eternal crown and the little things will roll off you! You will begin to get a picture of where you are headed. Yes, you are headed to paradise to be with Jesus. You will begin to understand why you are here! So that you can perform works of service, spread the good news of the Gospel, give testimony, and witness of Gods grace in your life. You will understand your purpose! It is to develop a heart for Jesus, to take up your Cross and let Jesus live out his life through you.

Finally, you will begin to see evidence of your good works because you will be motivated by Godly love not self-serving fear.

We will truly learn to value Gods word over our flesh. Why did you read this book? What do you truly value? What are you living for? What road are you headed down? Why are you here? What is your purpose? Where is the evidence of good works in your life?

The seeds to these questions lie in the fertile soil of our new hearts, the growth of our hearts lies in our willingness to seek God, through his word. The fruit of our labor will be our relationship with God as we journey through this place called earth, the reward of the eternal crown and Gods words to us when he asks us to account for our time and his response to our words is: "Well done good and faithful servant!" (Mt: 25:21 NIV)

I would like to share with you my personal creed and my personal prayer to God. I have these written in the front of my Bible and I cling to them. Every day I see what I value because I start my day with God, my creed and my prayer. My hope is that you will join me!

My Creed

This is my Bible. In it is the written word of God and the living word of Jesus Christ. God is spirit and Gods word is truth. In this Bible I will discover my heart and the person God created me to be. I believe I can do all things thru Christ, but first I must commit to know him thru his word, with all my heart, all my soul, and all of my mind. All of Gods power and grace is available to me thru My Bible! Everything I will ever need can be found in my Bible!

My Prayer

Jesus, you are my Lord and savior, you are the Christ, Divine and Holy, sovereign and full of grace. Jesus I give my heart and my life to you in hopes that I may reflect your glory to the world. I pray that I may be a lamp that shines from a hillside extolling your goodness and grace. I will love and pray for those who persecute me! I will take up my cross and seek to crucify my sinful nature! I will always strive to see with the eyes of my heart! In prayerful contemplation I will seek out the person, you have called me to be! Wherever opportunities arise, I will season conversation with the salt of your glory. Father I pray that you would grant me the courage and the wisdom to be a warrior for the Christian Heart! I pray that that you would give me the strength to balance my life between who I say I am and how I live this day! Amen

Chapter 11 Study Guide

Q1: What are you living for now and how do you plan to change it if at all?

Q2: What road have you been headed down and where are you going now?

Q3: Why are you here or specifically how do you think you can help bring others to know Christ?

Q4: What has your purpose in life been and how does that contrast with the new sense of purpose?

Q5: Discuss ways in which you can see evidence of good works in yours, your spouses or your groups ministries!

Chapter 12

A River Runs Through It

On November 15, 1992, I went to church to hear the Reverend Tim Croft. He was Minister of Myers Park Presbyterian Church in Charlotte, N.C. To hear Tim speak of God would leave me aching to know God better. One Sunday while I was still bound to the chains of my addiction, he spoke of the movie A River Runs Through It. The story moved me to obvious tears and in that sermon; Reverend Croft planted the seed for my new life. I would like to share this story with you because it made such a powerful impact on my life. I have watched that movie a hundred different times and every time I weep. I weep because I understand the brokenness, I weep because I know the struggle of trying to find myself. I weep because in the midst of the Pastor's family, in the movie, the boys missed an, oh so important relationship with their father and, more importantly, they missed the relationship with Christ, or so it seemed!

The story of A River Runs Through It is an exceptional story of the Reverend McLain's family life in Montana. Life in Montana, even for a pastor's family, can be ambiguous, broken, and incomplete. It was this way for the youngest son of the Reverend, Paul, who was a fun loving, hard living, arrogant, gambling, alcoholic young man. His older brother Norman was much his opposite and spent much of his time worrying and watching out for Paul. The movie would lead you to surmise that there was an infinite amount of unspoken human pain and brokenness between the family members, caused by the unfathomable ambiguities of their lives.

The boys seemed to have a deep separation from their parents. They did not communicate much, it seemed as though the father spent most of his time bringing other people to Christ. It seemed as though their mother was very quiet and reserved and left the training of the boys to her husband. It seemed as though the boys wanted to please their father, but could never quite reach him. He was there, but there did not seem to be a relationship. It seemed to be more of a disciplinary role. We did not see a picture of fun loving, playful activity amongst any of them. The only thing they seemed to enjoy doing together was fishing. They loved to fly-fish in the Big Blackfoot River in Montana, where they were raised. Yes, quite often they would wade out into the waters to fish. It was only there, in the river, that they seemed to encounter the peace of God. It was there that they laughed, smiled, and shared the best part of life, the relationship with each other.

The movie would have us believe that God was in the midst of that river and God's word, as the film suggests, is the power beneath the water. As the movie unfolds, we continue to see how broken and incomplete the lives of the brothers and father are. We see life's troubles unfold in many deep and painful ways, so deep, in fact, that they cannot seem to find a way to help each other even though they frantically want to.

Yet, when they return to the river to fish, when they return to God, seeking God while he can be found, calling upon him while he is near, they are somehow mysteriously healed and made whole. Even in the midst of their relevant brokenness, even in the midst of life's sorrow and uncertainty, even in the midst of their shared inability to be of any help to each other, they seem to be at peace at the river, where God is.

In the end of the movie my tears flowed because I, too, know the pain of not being able to help and heal the pain of those we love the most, and give them what they need the most.

I, too, know the pain of being hopelessly lost in a chronic addiction.

As the camera draws back and takes one last look at the phenomenal Big Blackfoot River which carves its way through the Montana countryside, we see the older brother Norman all alone, his family having all passed away, staring down into the waters of the Big Blackfoot River, almost as if he saw his father and brother there. I feel his pain and I see it on his face. In that final scene, we hear the daunting and painful last words:

" Eventually all things merge into one
  and a river runs through it,
  the river was cut by the world's great
  flood and runs over the rocks
from the basement of time,
on some of the rocks are timeless
raindrops, under the rocks are the words
  and some of the words are theirs,
I am haunted by the waters."

-A river runs through it-

In my journey all roads do merge into one and narrow is the gate that leads to life. When I envision the sadness of Norman, the older brother, my tears begin to flow. The story never tells us whether he knew God. The story leaves us with a picture of Norman sitting on a rock, listening and staring at the waters of the river. The picture projects an image of deep sadness and loss, the kind of pain one feels when you want to reach out and touch a loved one who is no longer with you. Yes, you can feel his anguish and his uncertainty. We are left wanting to take a hold of our loved ones and never let them go, to squeeze them ever so tightly and lavish are affections upon them while we can. I am left waxing rivers of tears and crying out to God to heal me from myself, to make me whole so that I can love completely. My heart aches for Norman and my heart aches for God. It leaves me with a surefooted discipline to seek God now, so that I can learn how to heal the brokenness in my life. It forces me to look in the mirror and learn what it is about my attitudes that can be changed and spurs me on to grow my heart for Jesus.

Friends, I want you to know that November 29, 1992 is the day I came to know Christ. Why is this so important? Because Reverend Croft did the greatest thing we can ever do while we are on this earth. He witnessed of Gods grace. He testified to the word of God and how knowing God can heal us and make us whole. Friends he planted the seed of desire in my heart. Within two weeks of that sermon I was crying out to God, I was ready to be transformed. How can we ever know the impact our witnessing may have on another? Moreover why do we allow fear of man to keep us from doing what we know in our hearts is right and good? Friends we can sweep one person at a time into the kingdom of God or even the multitudes, if and only if we reflect the Light of Jesus Christ in our walk and we witness of our transformation.

So it is, that God remains unchanging, always sovereign and full of love, discipline and grace and we must by our very new nature be ever changing in our walk to be like Christ! Yes we must all press on, we must never doubt our abilities and we must always work on our relationship with God because he truly is the best friend you will ever have and trust. I promise you that God will open doors you never dreamed would be available to you and he will mold you into the person you are called to be.

It is to God, all of my family, to Reverend Croft , Sophie Wood, and Will Sutterlin my business partner that I express my heartfelt gratitude. It is to the many others, too vast to name, that have lived exemplary, Godly lives, that I say thank you. To all of you who quietly inspired me and lifted me up, to find my calling in life, that I express my most sincere heartfelt gratitude. Yes, in your love for God, and in your willingness to give of yourself, you have indeed ensured that God's word would not return to him empty.

To all of you who have completed this book, I know your heart aches to know God better, always keep the faith, never, ever doubt God and his sovereign grace and remember we are made in the image of God. I urge you to seek God while he can be found, call upon him while he is near, and like me, God will guide you, like a river, to the way he would have you go!

Rest assured, I will be writing to you again! Until then, May the peace of Jesus Christ dwell in your hearts!

The End

Printed in the United States
by Baker & Taylor Publisher Services